WEND

# EASTER AND ASCENSION

# *Looking at*
# *EASTER &*
# *ASCENSION*

*Brian Haymes*

First published 1992
International Bible Reading Association
1020 Bristol Road
Selly Oak, Birmingham, B29 6LE


Copyright © IBRA 1992

*British Library Cataloguing-in-Publication Data:*
Haymes, Brian
    Looking at Easter and Ascension
    I. Title
    263


ISBN 0–7197–0781–1


The Bible quotations in this publication are from the
New Revised Standard Version (Collins Publishers) ©
1989, and used by permission.


Typeset by Avonset, Midsomer Norton, Bath, Avon
Printed and bound in Great Britain

To Ruby and Doris
two aunts in whose lives
I have glimpsed the risen Christ

# CONTENTS

Preface      9

1 By way of introduction      11

2 The resurrection in the Synoptic Gospels      24

3 The resurrection in the Fourth Gospel      42

4 Paul and the resurrection      53

5 Believing in the resurrection      69

6 Looking at ascension      87

# Preface

During the preparation of this book Joy Standen retired from her work with the IBRA. None the less she was willing to bring her editorial skills to bear on the text as it was prepared for the printers. All who have benefited from IBRA publications in recent years are indebted to her and I record, once more, my gratitude to her for her help, insight and kindness. To her, with Anne Hart, I offer thanks.

I am also grateful to Jenny Haymes for typing much of this book in its early stages and for many conversations on its theme.

Brian Haymes
December 1991

# 1
# By way of introduction

The cross and resurrection of Jesus stand at the centre of the Christian faith. As Paul said, 'If Christ has not been raised, your faith is futile' (1 Corinthians 15.17). Suppose that when the women came to Jesus' tomb on the Sunday morning after the Friday's killing they found his body, beaten, battered and covered with blood after the ordeal of lashing and crucifixion; suppose that Jesus had remained coldly dead; and, further, suppose that none of the disciples, Paul included, had any experience or encounter with Jesus after his death – that their last sight of him was as they laid him in the tomb. If all of these suppositions were correct, then there would be no Easter faith and Christianity as it is now proclaimed would not exist at all. Some people might have continued to remember Jesus was a notable teacher, perhaps a little too idealistic, but not without wisdom. Others might have been impressed with his kindness, his openness and compassion and adopted him as a role model – someone to be copied. Yet others might have admiration for someone actually willing to die for what he believed. These would have gladly claimed that Jesus was a good person, possibly the very best of men and women, although sadly wrong about God and certainly misguided in believing what he did about a kingdom breaking in. If we were to suppose any or all of this, then we would not have the Christian faith – we would only have the memory of a good and lovely person.

This short book then is about no small matter, for it is about the resurrection of Jesus – the heart of the Christian faith. It is that Jesus who lived a human life, was put to death, was buried and was raised to life by God. At the centre of our faith is a miracle, a work of God beyond the power of humankind to perform. Our faith is that God raised Jesus from the dead. This is an unusual claim to make, for the popular belief is that when you are dead you are dead. This is no modern slogan. It expresses the common sense, common experience of life. Resurrection must be something special, perhaps unique. If people today have doubts about it, or find the whole idea difficult to conceive and understand, then they are not alone. It has always been like that. Resurrection, empty tombs, direct encounters with those who have died are not normal. If there are big issues at stake here for the Christian faith, then there are also some very big questions. We shall try to get some of these into the open straight away.

## What is meant by resurrection – in particular, the resurrection of Jesus?

In John 11.1–44 we have the story of the raising of Lazarus, a close friend of Jesus. The Gospel writer almost goes out of his way to tell us that the man is dead, that he has been in the tomb, wrapped up in his shroud, for a number of days. The women are concerned that if the grave is opened there will be a bad smell. But Lazarus is called forth and comes out from the tomb. Is that resurrection? Yes, it is; but it is not what is at the heart of the resurrection of Jesus.

Presumably, if we take the story at face value, Lazarus' body eventually could take no more and he died again. No one pictures him living now. Lazarus' raising is the resuscitation of a corpse, a sign that manifests the glory of the One who is the resurrection and the life. Jesus' resurrection is something different.

Is the resurrection then a matter of a mysteriously empty tomb? The four Gospel writers, sometimes referred to as the four evangelists, all tell the story of this unexpected and amazing discovery. But the empty tomb, in itself, need not imply resurrection at all. Matthew's Gospel includes a reference to a rumour at the time, claiming that the tomb was empty because the disciples of Jesus had stolen his body (Matthew 27.62 – 66). Others have suggested that the grief-stricken women simply went to the wrong place. In other words, there may be several possible reasons given for the tradition of the empty tomb, none of which need imply that God raised Jesus from the dead. And anyway, if it is so important, why does Paul not make something of it?

Paul, of course, believes in the resurrection of Jesus from the dead because he has 'seen Jesus our Lord' (1 Corinthians 9.1). This is apostolic testimony, Paul believing himself to be the last of a long line of those to whom the risen Jesus has appeared. What are we to make of these claims? Are they visions? Are they particular kinds of intense religious experiences? How does Paul know it is Jesus who encounters him and not someone else – or even a figment of his imagination? How would you respond if your next-door neighbours called at your door tomorrow morning and told you that they had seen and met Jesus in their room last night? Does talk about resurrection rest on the particular claims of some New Testament people that they have met the Lord?

## What actually happened?

If talk about resurrection basically refers to having special experiences, then the historical questions of what happened at the empty tomb are not very important. However, the total witness of the New Testament implies that something happened not just in the minds and hearts of the disciples, but in history – an event took place. This is an important claim, but it is not without its difficulties. Suppose you had had a video camera set up, watching the tomb, what would a rerun of the tape show? Are we to take the accounts of the event in the four Gospels as straight historical records – or would that be to miss the real point? Does it matter, for example, that it is impossible to harmonise all the different details in the four accounts?

We could reply by saying that, while we believe that Jesus' resurrection is an event in history and that something definitely happened, we can say scarcely anything about it because of its utterly unique character. The resurrection of Jesus is not like the raising of Lazarus, for it is like nothing else on earth. To say this is to affirm the specialness of Jesus' resurrection but at the risk of making it almost beyond comprehension. How can we understand something that is totally unique? How can we know what it is if we have nothing with which to compare or relate it?

## What kind of God?

The resurrection is proclaimed as a miracle, that is, as a

14

work of God. The New Testament affirmation is not that Jesus the crucified somehow raised himself but that God raised Jesus from the dead.

Miracles are notoriously hard to define and they inevitably raise other questions for us, not least among these is: What kind of God is it who is said to act in the raising up of Jesus? In a world like ours, where we seek and find answers to most questions of fact by scientific methods of one kind or another, the idea of an interventionist God, who does things in a rather arbitrary and unaccountable way, is hard to grasp and believe. It can easily lead to a 'God of the gaps' mentality where, when our knowledge fails us, we attribute an event to God. However, this is tantamount to saying 'God' equals an explanation for what we otherwise do not know. Further, if we do think in this way, is there not a moral problem about a God who can do such a wonderful thing as raise Jesus from the dead but cannot, or will not, stop a famine, a car accident, or the atrocities of a war?

**Pursuing the questions**

These questions have not been raised just to be difficult, far less to trouble or destroy faith. They have been identified right at the start of this book because honesty demands it. In the light of our study we may have to question the questions, but there is no way in which we can ignore them. However, we must not think that we are the first people to have thought of them and faced them. The Easter faith has been lived, believed and suffered for many years before we came on the scene.

At the centre of New Testament faith is the death of Jesus on the cross, his burial and his resurrection. The greater part of this book will be concerned with examining the testimony of the New Testament writers whose work is the nearest we can come to the event. As we read their words we shall try to face, as honestly as we can, the questions that have been raised about the resurrection.

## Some background

The New Testament did not fall down to earth out of the blue; nor are the authors of the various books people without a context that has shaped their own thoughts and concepts. Jesus himself was a genuine person in history – flesh and blood, born a Jew – who used the language and imagery of his time and people. Therefore, we must remember that the New Testament stands on the shoulders of the Old. The story of God's ways with ancient Israel and with other nations is the historic context from which the record of Jesus and his resurrection comes. The God who raised Jesus from the dead is the God of Abraham, Isaac and Jacob, Sarah, Rachel and Esther, Elijah, Isaiah and Jeremiah, and on through history until BC becomes AD.

We have said that, in a crucial sense, the resurrection of Jesus is a unique event. But is there anything in the history and traditions of Israel, or in the very important time between the Old and the New Testaments, that would help us understand the message?

The idea, or doctrine, of resurrection is not a prominent one in the Old Testament. It only begins to come to the fore in the later books, that is, after the horrific and humiliating experience of exile. The nation of Israel had been divided and defeated. Humanly speaking the people were without hope. They and their God had become a laughing-stock among the nations. Some scholars suggest that it was while they were in Babylon that the Israelites took up imagery from their captor's religion, such as dying and rising, angels and demons, and began to employ this in their own stories and affirmations of faith. Certainly only after the exile do some themes, important for our understanding of the resurrection, begin to emerge.

Before that time there was the general belief that on death people's bodies returned to the dust of the soil and they lived on only in the existence of their family and the people of Israel. The Hebrew people seem to have thought of a person as a unity, not as a combination of body and soul. Thus, the end of the body was the end of life. There was the concept of *Sheol* (or the Pit) but it is not clear what was meant by that term. It was used in different ways – as a place of no movement, activity, hope or escape; as a place of the dead, especially the wicked; and as a place that is beyond the reign of God. There is no remembrance and praise of God in Sheol (Psalm 6.5). No one can even give thanks for God's faithfulness in the Pit (Isaiah 38.18). This meant that the rewards of living faithfully and trustingly in the covenant were understood to be long life and length of days (Psalm 21.4).

The trouble with that view of life is that it does not always fit the facts. The good sometimes die young, and the unrighteous can succeed very well in the world's terms. It may be that the children suffer for their parents' sins, paying the penalty for many generations, but this is not always the case. The question at issue here is of God's justice and

17

righteousness. The book of Job stands in constant challenge to any easy theory about rewards and punishments in this life. It was in the context of the problem of suffering, especially of unjust suffering, that resurrection came to be considered. It may well be that in exile Israel found the language and imagery that enabled the people to affirm faith in the ultimate victorious purposes of God.

Certainly the experience of being taken into Babylon, of being surprised there by God's presence, led to great affirmations of God's sovereign rule in all history (Psalm 139.7 – 8). Although the nations had poured scorn on little Israel and her God in the days of defeat, her people came to believe in a more profound understanding of God and his purposes. However, even though they returned to rebuild Jerusalem and were given opportunity to recover their national sense of purpose, it still left their desperate cry for the vindication of the righteous in the light of personal disaster ringing in the ears.

We must not imagine that the people of Israel then settled down to think out their own view on resurrection. There never was just one understanding of resurrection and life after death. For example, we know from the Gospels that Pharisees and Sadducees held different views. The Sadducees did not believe in resurrection (Mark 12.18) for they kept their teaching strictly to the five books of Moses (Genesis, Exodus, Leviticus, Numbers and Deuteronomy) where they found no reference to resurrection. The Pharisees on the other hand did not keep so strictly to these books and were willing to let their thoughts develop. Thus they came to believe in life after death, resurrection, angels and demons. Much of this imagery became current in Palestine in the period between the Old and New Testaments. With these ideas the people gave expression to their faith that God is sovereign, his purposes will be completed and he will never abandon his people. Again some scholars suggest that after the exile the language of God's covenant care for Israel was recast and found new expression in the language of resurrection.

Is it possible to identify the main ideas and concepts about resurrection and life after death that were current in the period prior to the birth of Jesus for it is this time that provides the context for his ministry? Although even the basic ideas and the developments that were taking place are far from clear, the following can be said:

Increasing attention was being given to judgement and vindication. Increasingly in the later Jewish Scriptures there emerged the idea of the court of heaven with God taking council (Job 1.6). God's judgements were made and declared not simply within history but also in the life to come (Daniel 12.1–3). There is clearly some correspondence between the life lived on earth and the judgement eventually received. So there emerged the concept of the general resurrection where the wicked are left to live in *Gehenna*, a place of fire and punishment, while the righteous will dwell in light. It was in this sense that the Pharisees expected the resurrection of the just. What appeared to be manifest injustices in this life would be put right by God.

It is not surprising, therefore, to find in the imagery of much apocalyptic writing of the time a picture of a vast struggle of cosmic proportions going on in history. Satan is presented as directly challenging the will and claim of God. But the people of God were encouraged to trust God and live faithfully because God's purposes would eventually triumph and the faithful would receive their reward. Daniel 7, with its reference to one like a son of man (human being) coming on the clouds of heaven, creating a kingdom where God fulfils all the longing of the righteous, is a powerful expression of this theme. In the time before the birth of Jesus there occurred what is called the Maccabean Revolt, when strongly-committed Jews lived and died for their faith. The question about the righteous became more and more intense. Clearly, as the Maccabees were defeated, the wrong people were dying. There was no simple justice of God in this life. Yet the belief, that surely the just will be vindicated and God's will will be done, grew stronger.

But, will that vindication and triumph be something that happens in the world's history? Or will it be beyond history, in a new creation of God? Different kinds of resurrection imagery belong with Israel's life. Take, for example, the powerful picture of the valley of dry bones and the spirit coming and clothing the skeletons with flesh in Ezekiel 37.1–14. This theme of corporate renewal, proclaimed while the nation was defeated and in exile, shares an earlier emphasis that Israel will live on in her children. But there come more personal, individual prospects and sometimes the imagery is of this flesh-and-blood world transformed, while at other times it is 'other worldly'.

There is some evidence in the Apocrypha (books covering the years between the Old and New Testaments) of the belief in the immortality of the soul. The Hebrews looked upon a human being as a unity, not a being with several parts. The Hebrew word, *nephesh* – usually translated 'soul' – means a living being, distinct from God. However, among Greeks there was a dualism – human life was thought of as body and soul. The material body was said to pass away but the soul was immortal. Although there is evidence of this kind of belief in the Apocrypha, the Jews did not traditionally hold with such dualism. For them, there was no existence that was not bodily existence (1 Corinthians 15.44), but it is difficult to be clear and dogmatic about these ideas. The point is that all these and others as well were 'available' at the time of Jesus.

One other theme that was certainly in the literature of the time before Jesus – especially during the period of the Maccabean revolt – was that of divine intervention. In this emphasis was placed on certain figures – the Messiah, the Son of Man, the return of Elijah. There was an expectancy that something new and wonderful, aweful and glorious, was about to happen. God would intervene in human history, to establish his kingdom, to bring judgement and vindication for his people.

All of this was the context for Jesus' ministry. There was no uniformity of thought and some of the ideas were far from clear. At the centre of it all was the massive belief that the God of Israel would come in a mighty act of deliverance which would mean a thorough transformation, breaking out of the limitations of earthly existence and death. The Lord would come and save his people.

### The plan of the book

In the following chapters we shall 'listen' to the various voices of the New Testament. They do not all speak in the same tones and with the same emphases but they all have the belief that they are witnesses giving testimony to the great work of God.

We shall begin in chapter 2 with the **Synoptic Gospels** (Matthew, Mark and Luke) before turning in chapter 3 to the Easter narratives in **John**. We shall not attempt to harmonise the story they tell or to reconcile the differences. Rather, we shall treat them as the witnesses they are, passing on their testimony in their own way. Behind each of the four Gospels there stands a community which has made its own contribution to what is remembered of the story of Jesus. For simplicity's sake, in this book, we shall refer to the authors of the Gospels as Matthew, Mark, Luke and John.

Then, in chapter 4, we shall look at some of the writings of **Paul**. Written before the Gospels these are the earliest writings we have about the resurrection. In chapter 5 we shall consider in more depth various questions raised about believing in the resurrection before turning to the ascension of Jesus in chapter 6.

## A prayer

O gracious God, our hope and our refuge, God of life and resurrection, you have opened your heart to the world in Jesus. We thank you for standing by us in our need, with us in our poverty, among us in our struggles. Grant us grace that we may love you with all our minds, and in loving come to a deeper understanding, and with understanding to a deeper trust and open faith in your risen presence and power; through Jesus Christ our Lord. Amen.

**Some questions and suggestions for further thought**

1  Invite someone who is not a Christian believer to talk through with you some of the questions you and he/she have about the resurrection of Jesus.

2  People send and receive many Christmas cards. Think of a few people to whom you would particularly like to give Easter greetings and send them a card or letter.

3  Recall any experience which you would identify as an encounter with the living Christ. Reflect on it and its significance for your life, and give thanks to God.

4  Make your own list of questions and issues about Easter and the resurrection which you hope this book might help you to face. Keep it as a check-list as you read the next four chapters.

# 2

# The resurrection in the Synoptic Gospels

The Synoptic Gospels are Matthew Mark and Luke. *'Synoptic'* comes from a Greek word which means 'seeing together', and it is applied to these three Gospels because they look so alike. It has been calculated that the majority of Mark is word for word in Matthew, and about half of Mark is in Luke. You can easily check this by comparing the story of Jesus healing a man with a dreaded skin-disease (leprosy) in Matthew 8.1–4, Mark 1.40–45 and Luke 5.12–16. Another illustration is the story about Jesus in a controversy over the Sabbath in Matthew 12.1–8, Mark 2.23–28 and Luke 6.1–5.

Although these three Gospels are so alike in their order and language, such that most scholars believed Mark was written first and then used by Matthew and Luke, they are not in fact identical. There are differences, some only slight but together they help us see that the Gospel writers were responding to their own situations. So Matthew, writing out of a Jewish Christian community, often quotes the Old Testament; Mark, possibly written in Rome during the first period of direct persecution of Christians, emphasises the sufferings of Christ; while Luke, a Gentile and missionary companion of Paul, tells the story of Jesus to include all people, even the despised, such as the poor, women, and Samaritans.

The three Gospels are the same – yet different. It is especially in the differences that we can detect the particular theological insights of the writers as they try to tell the all-important story of Jesus in their own context. They all tell the story of the resurrection on Easter Day, but they do not tell it in the same manner. We shall look at each of their accounts in turn.

The three Synoptic Gospel writers proclaim the empty tomb. In chapter 1 we said that it was impossible to harmonise all the accounts of the empty tomb. In fact, it is not just impossible, it is highly undesirable if the differences can give us clues into what the writers meant by the accounts they give.

### The stone is rolled away   Mark 16.1 – 8

We begin with Mark because it is generally held to be the first of the Gospels to be written. It is difficult to be precise and confident about our knowledge of the community from which the Gospels separately come but it is possible that Mark's community was in Rome, at the time of Nero's persecution when Peter and Paul are said to have been martyred. When faith is hard pressed then comfort is needed. What is required is no easy, cheap comfort that gives nothing at all. Rather, what is needed is the strength-giving word of the gospel. This certainly includes suffering for the Lord, and perplexity and misunderstanding for the disciples. But believing the gospel means having faith in the triumph of God, not in spite of suffering, but through it. These are the themes in Mark's story of Jesus.

In most modern versions of Mark's account of the resurrection there is a break after verse 8 – the women 'said nothing to anyone, for they were afraid'. The best and most trustworthy Greek manuscripts of the Gospel end there. It seems so odd to finish like that; but we shall look at this issue later, when we have followed the story through.

Mark begins in 16.1–4 with the discovery of the empty tomb by the women. Generally, in the world of that time, women were not taken seriously as witnesses of anything. Mark mentions three women and significantly one of them is Mary Magdalene – the only one mentioned in all the four Gospel accounts. The fact that she is the only consistent witness is a strong argument, historically, that she is the one who discovered the empty tomb.

The women are said to have come to the tomb to perform the last burial rites. Normally, anointing the body would be performed quickly because of the effect of the hot climate. However, in the case of Jesus, the women had to delay doing this task because of the Sabbath. Perhaps Mark's reference to the burial rites is his strong assertion of the unquestionable reality of Jesus' death, the particular loyalty of these women to him, and the fact that by coming to embalm him they showed that they did not expect resurrection at all.

Mark seems to go out of his way to emphasise the time – 'when the Sabbath was over' and 'the first day of the week' (verses 1–2). It appears odd that the women only raise the question of moving the great stone that seals the tomb after they have set out. But perhaps this is one of Mark's ways of showing how unexpected the resurrection of Jesus was. On arriving at the tomb they find that the stone has been moved already. It is remarkable how restrained Mark's language is here. The open tomb does not produce amazement, and it certainly does not lead to faith in the resurrection of Jesus. There is no immediate explanation of what has happened.

The women enter the tomb and there see a young man, wearing a white robe, the symbol of heaven. He is sitting on the right side. Does this reflect Mark 12.36 and 14.62? So far nothing has been said about the presence or absence of Jesus' body, but we are told that the women are alarmed (verse 5). The word used here is a strong one, implying that the women realised that this was not any young man but God's messenger. It is the first indication of divine action.

Verse 6 brings us to the heart of the matter. The messenger first tells the women not to be alarmed – that itself would be a word for Mark's own distressed community. 'Being alarmed' or 'afraid' is a common biblical response to an encounter with God. Then comes the decisive message. The messenger does not ask them but tells them that they are 'looking for Jesus of Nazareth, who was crucified'. The details underline the identity of the One who is the subject of the message. Then the messenger says, 'He has been raised; he is not here.' God's action now comes plainly to the fore; he has intervened when all appeared lost. The young man goes on to invite the women to see the place where Jesus had been laid. In this way we are told that the tomb is indeed empty.

But notice how Mark has put all this. First comes the proclamation of resurrection – 'he has been raised'; then follows the word about the absence of the body – 'he is not here'. God's action precedes everything else. There is no other explanation. It is as if Mark is saying, 'Jesus has been raised. He cannot be here. You can come and see that for yourself.'

This announcement of the resurrection is immediately followed by instruction. The women are to tell the disciples – and Peter gets a special mention – that Jesus has gone ahead to Galilee. There they will see him as he said (Mark 14.28). Just the mention of Peter is enough to recall his boast and his denial (see Mark 14.29 – 31, 66 – 72). He is chief among those who failed at the time of trial. So Jesus' meeting with the disciples in Galilee, at the place where the Gospel began and where much of the teaching on discipleship was given, is in marked distinction from his abandonment. The risen Christ will come again to meet the failures. Those who forsake Jesus will not find themselves forsaken by him. In this encounter with Christ at the place of discipleship the significance of the empty tomb and the message of the young man will be made clear.

Mark says that the women went out from the tomb, in terror and amazement. Such a response is common in Mark where the followers of Jesus are often pictured as being uncomprehending and fearful. In fact they did not pass the message on: 'they said nothing to anyone, for they were afraid' (verse 8).

And that is how the best manuscripts of Mark's Gospel ends. Did Mark mean this to be the conclusion? There is no record in any of the Gospel accounts of the empty tomb producing faith in itself. The full meaning of 'God has raised him' is not dependent on the tomb being empty at all. So is Mark being consistent with the rest of his Gospel in pointing to the blindness, fear and lack of understanding of the disciples until their eyes are opened? Or was the manuscript damaged here and the original ending lost? Who can tell?

### The longer ending   Mark 16.9 – 20

Certainly verses 9 – 20 have a different feel about them, as if they come from another hand. For example, verse 9 has 'he rose' whereas the other accounts accentuate the fact that Jesus was raised by divine initiative. Again, verse 10 mentions the women 'mourning and weeping', words used in Scripture to describe the appropriate behaviour at a funeral, but they are not used at all by the other Gospel writers. Only here does Jesus reproach the disciples 'for their lack of faith and stubbornness' in the face of the resurrection message (see verse 14). All this, together with an ascension story (verse 19) different from that in Luke, suggests that an independent tradition is being used here.

This ending of Mark contains references of a brief nature to stories which appear in other Gospels. For example, verse 12 echoes the two on the road to Emmaus in Luke 24.13 – 35. The reference to baptism in verses 15 – 16 may be linked with Matthew 28.19; and, in verse 18, there is reference to spectacular gifts which are all mentioned in Acts, apart from drinking deadly things (poison) without harm.

Jesus' reproach of the disciples' stubborn slowness to believe is followed by his calling them into service. The steady theme of the Messiah who suffers is here replaced by the vision of One who makes his way triumphantly into and through the world in the Church's proclamation of the gospel. The unbelief of the world is not then conquered by the resurrection in itself but by obedient witness to the Christ of God.

The longer ending includes Christ's ascension, which is the enthronement of the Easter King; and this Gospel concludes with the missionary task of the disciples. In these terms, the objective of God's raising of Jesus is the proclamation of the gospel in the world. The frail, sometimes pathetic disciples, called again after their cowardliness into service, are the sharers in that task. Only the risen Christ himself could have overcome their unbelief and fear.

We leave Mark's Gospel here for the moment. The main themes we have encountered in 16.1–8 are: resurrection as God's raising up of the dead Jesus; the unexpectedness of this for the disciples; the empty tomb; and the promise that Jesus will meet with his otherwise dispirited and failed followers. We now move on to Matthew.


### The account in Matthew
#### Matthew 27.62 – 66; 28.1 – 20

Matthew, with its many Old Testament quotations, is the most Jewish of the Synoptic Gospels. However, it is not easy to be clear what the exact connection with Judaism is. Is it that this Gospel is a Jewish-Christian interpretation of Jesus, many members of the Church being Jews who have become Christians? Or does the Gospel show that, for all its Jewish origins, Christianity has moved to an independent identity? There is some evidence that around the year AD 80 Jewish leaders began to ban Christians from worship in the synagogue. Perhaps the situation is that, for all its roots in the Old Testament, the Church now believes itself to be the true Israel. As such it knows some painful unease in its relations with Judaism, and understands its mission as being not just to Israel alone but to all nations.

Matthew seems to know Mark's shorter ending and

uses it. But he has some extra material in two sections and we shall begin with these.

## A guard for the grave   Matthew 27.62 – 66

In Jewish thinking resurrection must mean 'from the grave'. A grave that had a body in it would be enough to deny all talk about resurrection. However, if the tomb of Jesus were empty, that, of itself, need not imply resurrection. The body could have been stolen, and this is the possibility, put about as rumour, that Matthew now faces.

On the day after the death and burial of Jesus, which would be the Sabbath, the Jewish leaders go to Pilate to have the tomb made secure. Somehow it is hard to believe this. It is in complete contrast to John 18.28 where they would not approach Pilate's dwelling for fear of becoming ritually unclean. The very way in which Matthew writes makes the Jews appear as 'outsiders'. They request that the tomb be made 'secure' – a word that is used three times in these verses. If the rumour should get out that Jesus has been raised, as he said he would be, then the second deception would be worse than the first – the claim that Jesus is the promised Messiah.

Pilate tells the Jews to look after this themselves – they must make the grave as secure as they can. There may be a touch of irony here, implying that such an idea is ridiculous from the start. However, they do go and secure the stone. This might well have been done by putting slime or wax into the cracks or joints between the stone and the tomb entrance and then impressing a seal in the wax (see Daniel 6.17).

The whole idea – that disciples who had fled in terror from Jerusalem should plan within hours of the execution to come and retrieve the body by theft – seems far-fetched. But Matthew's community knows this rumour is about and is intent on silencing it. Once again we note that the fact of the empty tomb may not be disputed, only its explanation.

## The rumour is started   Matthew 28.11–15

After Matthew has told the story of the resurrection, in which the guards were so affected that they shook and became like dead men (verse 4), he now tells about the origin and spread of a malicious rumour.

Faced with the empty tomb the guards report to the chief priests, those who had appointed them to the task of securing and keeping safe the tomb. As at the beginning of the passion story, two things happen: the chief priests and elders take counsel together and try to solve their problem with money. They require the guards to lie, promising that they will keep them out of trouble should Pilate get to hear of it. All this is too hard to believe. To admit that they slept on duty would be tantamount to hastening their own severe punishment. And how would Pilate be able, if he wanted, to hush the whole thing up?

But Matthew says that the soldiers accepted the bribe and began to spread the false rumour around, a rumour still current in the days when this Gospel was written. The Jews then are pictured as those who are teaching a lie, and this is consistent with their blind opposition to the work of God. There is indeed an anti-Jewish tone to Matthew's writing here. His purpose is not to 'prove' the resurrection – the empty tomb cannot do that.

However, he does want to show that the theft of the body of Jesus is not simply highly improbable but just not true. Whatever else happened, the tomb was not empty because the body of Jesus was stolen.

### The women at the tomb   Matthew 28.1–10

Most scholars see evidence in these verses both of Matthew following Mark's account and his developing of it. Again we notice that the resurrection itself is not witnessed or described by anyone. Later apocryphal Gospel writers were not so reticent and let their imaginations run wild.

When do the two women (not three as in Mark) come to the tomb? Some interpreters take the phrase 'after the Sabbath' to mean after 6.00 pm, in the evening on the Saturday. The women have not come to do anything to the body. They are there to sit and watch. Were they expecting anything?

Whatever the women expect, they are taken aback by what happens. Using apocalyptic language Matthew says that an earthquake shakes the ground, and an angel of the Lord comes down from heaven and moves the stone. The angel is described in fuller detail than in Mark. Imagery of earthquakes and angels of the Lord, such as found here, is often used eschatologically – that is, of speaking of the end of all things.

The effect of all this on the guards is immediate. They lose control, shake and become like dead men. How ironic! They were meant to be the living guarding the dead! Verses 2 – 4 are very characteristic of this Gospel in language and style. Matthew is interpreting Mark with apocalyptic imagery. As such, he is not giving new information so much as interpreting the fearful and wonderful event.

The angel tells the women not to be afraid and says that he knows who they are looking for. It is not for them to be paralysed like the guards. Then there is a slight but significant change from Mark's wording. The angel first tells the women that Jesus is not here, and then that he is risen. The empty tomb is seen to have a message after all. The women are then sent quickly to tell the 'disciples' – a term in Matthew that means a larger group than the twelve. Perhaps that is why Peter is not mentioned.

So, without going into the tomb, the women leave filled with fear and great joy. In the New Testament the resurrection is often a cause for joy (see Luke 24.52 and John 16.20). They go as they have been commanded and are met by Jesus. This is not in Mark but may relate to the tradition found in John 20.11–18. The women fall in worship, symbolised in grasping Jesus' feet. Again they are told not to be afraid but to go and tell the 'brothers' the good news. 'Brothers' is at first a surprising word until we remember Matthew 12.49.

When we contrast Matthew with Mark we notice that there is slightly more stress in Matthew on the resurrection as an objective event, but still no one actually witnesses it. The guards are unconscious and the women only later see the risen One. However, establishing that the tomb is empty is part of the announcement of resurrection in Matthew. His account is a strong word of proclamation and an invitation to faith.

We shall leave the concluding verses of Matthew's Gospel until the last chapter, and now move on to Luke.

## The account in Luke    Luke 24.1– 43

If Matthew is the Gospel with a Jewish emphasis, then Luke is the one for Gentiles (non-Jews). The author is ready to explain aspects of Jewish life in the story of Jesus to help his readers. He writes with great care and style, and includes some of the most beautiful of verses which are found only in this Gospel. For example, the story of the two on the road to Emmaus is not only the longest but also the most carefully written of all the resurrection stories.

Luke's community knows what it is to live in a hostile environment. He seems to have a sympathy for outsiders of all kinds – Samaritans, the poor, women, Gentiles and tax-collectors, for example. His is a Gospel full of joy and hope. Gentile though he is, he sees Jerusalem as the centre from which the gospel of Jesus spreads out to all the known world, especially to Rome.

## Finding the empty tomb    Luke 24.1– 12

Luke follows Mark's account of Easter morning but not without some significant changes. There seems to be a more obvious connection between the burial and resurrection stories here. For example, verse 1 mentions the spices which the women – unnamed at this point – had previously prepared (Luke 23.56). This small piece of information implies the women's devotion to Jesus and also the fact that, as in the other accounts, no one expected resurrection at all.

Luke does not mentioned any worries the women might have about who will roll away the stone. Such things detract from his central point – namely, that when the women went into the tomb, they did not find the body of Jesus. This is the fact Luke wants to assert. It would be important for his Gentile readers to grasp that the women did not have a vision but that they actually went into the place of the dead Jesus and found it empty. The women are perplexed and the angels come to interpret.

There are two 'men' in Luke's account, both in dazzling clothes. In his story of the transfiguration (Luke 9.28 – 36) and at the ascension (Acts 1.10) two men of similar description are present and they have the task of interpreting the experience to the witnesses. The women react with awe and fear, and they keep their eyes to the ground (verse 5). They are asked why they are looking for Jesus in a place like this. The question has the hint of an implied rebuke – had they not listened carefully enough to Jesus' own teaching? Luke tells how the 'men' recall what Jesus had said in Galilee about his passion and resurrection (verses 6–7). For Luke, Galilee will not be a place of return for resurrection experiences; rather, these will all centre on or about Jerusalem before the gospel is spread into all the world. Galilee is remembered as a place of prophecy; and Easter is the unlocking of the great mystery surrounding the fact that the Son of Man must suffer, be crucified and buried.

Luke says that the women remember and go straight away to tell the eleven and the other disciples. With their recalling of the words of Jesus the empty tomb becomes comprehensible. Their perplexity is gone, and their witness begins without their experiencing any resurrection appearance.

Now the names are given of three women, but Luke mentions that there are also others. They keep on telling the apostles but are not believed. It has been suggested that what Luke is doing here is maintaining the independency of the women's testimony. In the world of that time women were not reckoned to be reliable witnesses. Luke's Gentile readers would know that. When Peter goes to check the story, he finds the tomb empty and returns home 'amazed'. This is not yet the full Easter faith. The empty tomb produces amazement and puzzlement. But the full Easter faith can only be given by the risen Christ, and his encounter with the disciples is yet to come.

### The meal at Emmaus   Luke 24.13 – 35

This is by far the longest single resurrection story and one of the most beautiful. Some of the major themes in Luke's theology are very evident.

It all happens on the evening of Easter Day. Two members of the wider circle of disciples are journeying home. They are in some despair and perplexity as they discuss the events of the last few days. Then a stranger joins them. He is unrecognised but becomes their companion on the way. When he asks what they are discussing, they are astonished at his question, for they are so absorbed in what has happened to Jesus. Where has this stranger been the last few days?!

Their reply to Jesus has three important parts. First, they tell how they have been talking about Jesus from Nazareth, the prophet, who had some fame among the people but was handed over by the chief priests to the authorities and was crucified. Then, they speak of their own disappointed hopes. They had followed this Jesus, believing that he would be the one to redeem his people, but all they have now is their shattered dreams because Jesus is gone. Lastly, they tell the stranger that it is now the third day after these events. They tell how some women found the tomb empty and how they had a message from angels that he was alive, but all that some of the disciples could do was confirm that the tomb was empty. (All this is just a summary of Luke 24.1–12.)

Here again is that important difference we have noted before – the difference between the message of the empty tomb and the full resurrection faith. These two journeying home to Emmaus knew that the tomb was empty but they were unable to see Jesus.

Jesus now speaks and challenges their slowness to believe. He suggests that Jesus' death was not a disaster, rather it was necessary that the Christ must suffer – this is a strong theme in Luke. If they had understood the Scriptures aright they would have realised all this. Jesus is the Christ, not in spite of his suffering death, but because of it.

The stranger is persuaded to stay for a meal. It is while they are at table, sharing an ordinary meal, that the most wonderful thing happens. Jesus takes bread, blesses it, breaks it, and gives it to them. The reader is reminded of the Last Supper in the Upper Room although these two disciples were not among those present then.

The two disciples race back to Jerusalem, the city they had left with shattered hopes. Now they return with the message – Jesus really is risen! They have their testimony to the conversation about the Scriptures and how he was known in the breaking of the bread.

An important feature of Luke's Gospel is the way Jesus shared meals with all kinds of people. His mixing and eating with sinners is a sign of the presence of

God's kingdom. Here Luke is affirming that the combination of reading Scripture and the breaking of bread leads to a moment of resurrection awareness by the disciples. The implication is that this was not just true then but it can happen for us also. Resurrection is known in the fellowship of the risen Christ with his people.

**Some first reflections**

These are first reflections because we shall come to pursue some of the issues raised here later, in chapter 5. The main points can be summarised in this way. It is the testimony of the Synoptic Gospels that:

No one expected anything on the third day except that the body of Jesus would be in the tomb where it had been left. Therefore, what the women found was totally unexpected.

The tomb was empty. Matthew and Luke seem to stress the objectivity of this more than Mark, but there is no doubt about the matter for any of them.

The fact that the tomb was empty is not put down to any human possibility; it is a miracle, a work of God. The tomb would not be empty if God had not acted.

The empty tomb itself does not produce resurrection faith. Rather, initially it produces perplexity and even despair. However, the Synoptic Gospels also tell of appearances of the risen Jesus, appearances that would be impossible if the tomb had a body in it. It is these appearances that lead the disciples to a fuller realisation of the Easter faith and message.

39

Those who receive the message are implicitly charged with proclaiming it. That the Lord is risen is indeed good news to tell.

## A prayer

O God, you know in Jesus the aweful agony and reality of death, we praise you for the word of resurrection life. We thank you for those women, disciples and apostles who, scorning ridicule, told of what they had seen and whom they had met. For the word of your gospel, for every experience of your living presence, we worship and praise your name. Amen.

## Some questions and suggestions for further thought

1 Take part in a 'role play' free discussion based on the women returning from the tomb to tell the disciples that the grave is empty. Remember that the women would be counted as doubtful witnesses.

2 In what ways does the telling of the resurrection story by Matthew, Mark and Luke reflect the needs of the congregations to which they were writing? You will find some help for this in the opening paragraphs of chapters 2, 3 and 4 of *Looking at the Cross* (published by IBRA). Alternatively, ask your minister for some help or consult a Bible Dictionary.

3 The Emmaus Road story (Luke 24.13 – 35) links inevitably in our minds with Holy Communion or the Eucharist. Recall when one of these services, or a particular meal, was special to you.

4 For people, like the Synoptic Gospel writers, the Jewish context from which the Church came was very important. In this context the empty tomb was essential to resurrection belief. Do you think it is so for us today?

# 3

# The resurrection in the Fourth Gospel

John's Gospel is almost certainly the last of the four to be written. The Christian Church had spread over an increasingly wide geographical area, leaving its Jewish roots and heading deep into Gentile territory.

Such growth was not without its problems. John wrote his Gospel with Christian readers in mind, conscious that they were facing misunderstanding and opposition. But he did not write only for Christians. He states his overall purpose very clearly: 'These are written so that you may come to believe that Jesus is the Messiah, the Son of God, and that through believing you may have life in his name' (John 20.31). There is no doubt that Jesus Christ is the very centre of this Gospel and that John is concerned both with opponents who deny Jesus' divinity and others who refuse to accept his humanity.

John writes with directness to drive home his message. The challenge is to believe or perish, to receive life or death, to live in the light or darkness. There is no middle ground in John's world and the crucial factor is response to Jesus.

It is often argued that Ephesus is the 'home' for the Fourth Gospel. There was hostility to the Christian Church in that city which was Greek and, therefore, Gentile, although there was a strong Jewish group and a continuing number of disciples of John the Baptist (see Acts 19.1–7). It was what we now call a pluralistic culture with many religions, some of which would have stood in opposition to Christianity. But John and his community were convinced that Jesus alone was 'the way, the truth, and the life' (John 14.6).

John 20 and 21 are this Gospel writer's account of the resurrection. Chapter 20 reports the tradition of the empty tomb and the appearances in Jerusalem, while chapter 21 recounts the tradition of appearances in Galilee. Some think that this last chapter belongs with a second edition of the Gospel and comes from another hand. Either way, this Gospel sets forth Jesus as the One who won a great victory in the cross, a place of darkness and the place where darkness is vanquished. The resurrection of Jesus is not so much the victory itself as its inevitable result.

### Mary and the disciples at the tomb    John 20.1–10

Once again a Gospel writer tells us that Mary Magdalene came to the tomb early, while it was still dark. She is the only woman who appears consistently in the Easter Day narratives. John gives no reason for her visit and mentions, in a rather flat phrase, that 'the stone had been removed from the tomb' (verse 1). Perhaps John does not dwell on this because he wants nothing to detract from the great discovery.

Mary is distressed at what she finds. Again there is no possible preparation for this. She runs to Peter and the 'other disciple, the one Jesus loved' – usually referred to as the beloved disciple – and tells them, 'They have taken the Lord out of the tomb, and we do not know where they have laid him' (verse 2). Who 'they' are we can only guess. Mary speaks as if Jesus' body has been stolen.

Peter and the other disciple race to the tomb, with the beloved disciple arriving first. He looks into the grave and sees the linen wrappings but does not go in. There is no mention of angels at this time.

Then Peter arrives and enters the tomb. He sees the linen wrappings. The napkin is singled out for detail, rolled up carefully in its place. Clearly this is no robbery. Then the other disciple enters, he sees and believes. We are not told the precise content of that belief but he has come to faith on the basis of the empty tomb, without any appearance of the risen Jesus. It may be that John is picturing the beloved disciple as a kind of example of those who have not seen, yet have come to believe (see John 20.29).

Actually, there has been no direct reference to resurrection thus far. The tomb is empty. Mary has drawn the wrong conclusion, but the beloved disciple has 'seen' and believed. In verse 9, John says what the content of that belief is – namely, that Jesus must rise from the dead. Like Luke, John links this perception with a true understanding of the Scriptures.

## The Lord appears to Mary   John 20.11–18

The Gospel account now moves back to Mary. She stays outside the tomb weeping, giving expression to her grief – or possibly her wrath and anger that go with bereavement. Through her tears she peers into the tomb. John – perhaps he is following one of the traditions – tells us that two angels are present, seated where Jesus lay. The receiving of the message is at the heart of the experience, confirming and explaining the painful problem of the empty tomb. But, unlike the tradition, John does not speak of Mary possessed by fear. When she is asked why she is weeping, she repeats her distress that the body of Jesus has been taken. It does not occur to her to think that he might be risen.

The angels fade from the story and Jesus appears. Mary does not recognise him. Only slowly does the truth dawn. She is asked again why she is weeping, but also for whom she is looking. She thinks it is a gardener speaking to her. Perhaps he will know what has been done with the body of Jesus. Then Jesus says, 'Mary!' The moment of recognition is the calling and hearing of her name. Personal relations matter a great deal in the Fourth Gospel's understanding of Jesus. Does not the good shepherd call his own by name; do they not hear his voice and respond (see John 10.3 – 5)?

So Mary turns to face Jesus. 'Rabbouni' she answers. This is a lengthened form of 'rabbi' which John tells us means 'Teacher', except that the longer form carries deep respect and deference.

Mary Magdalene moves to touch Jesus but is told not to. He has not yet ascended to the Father. It is not that Jesus cannot be touched. The strong Jewish influences in John would have stressed the resurrection of the body. Rather, something new has happened and that is what is to be acknowledged and received. This is no time for Mary, or any disciple, to try to cling on to the flesh of Jesus.

Jesus is ascending to his Father and theirs, to his God and theirs – that is what she must tell his 'brothers'. John's Gospel does not have an account of an ascension separate from resurrection as does Luke's. These resurrection appearances are but pauses in the single movement from cross to glory. Only in this sense has Jesus not yet ascended. The fact is that he is already going to the Father. A new epoch, the age of resurrection, has already begun and the Spirit will soon be given.

So Mary becomes the first witness – 'I have seen the Lord,' she says.


## Thomas, doubting and believing   John 20.19 – 29

As in Luke, so in John we have an account of the risen Lord coming to the disciples on the evening of Easter Day. The fact that, in verse 19 and again in verse 26, it is recorded that the disciples are gathered together on Sunday evening may suggest that in John's community there was a regular congregational meeting in which Christ makes his presence known. The doors are locked and so the miraculous nature of Jesus' coming is underlined. Jesus stands in their midst and gives the word of peace, the normal greeting that this time must have been full of abnormal significance.

Jesus shows his hands and side (verse 20). This is indeed the same one who was cruelly crucified. The disciples respond with joy when they see the Lord. Again Jesus speaks the word of peace, and then words of commission: 'As the Father has sent me, so I send you' (verse 21). We are not told which of the disciples are present and it does not matter because these disciples stand for all the members of the Church past, present, and to come. They carry on the mission of Christ which he himself received from the Father. The Church does not have a mission of its own; its privilege is to share the mission of Christ.

Jesus breathes on them. Is there an echo here of Genesis 2.7 when God first breathed the breath of life into human beings? The same word for 'breathed' is used in the Greek translation of the Old Testament, the *Septuagint*, in Ezekiel 37.9, the story of the coming to life of the valley of dry bones. Is this John's way of talking of the new creation? And the disciples receive Holy Spirit – the definite article is absent in the Greek. In John 7.39 we are told that the Spirit has not yet been given because Jesus is not yet glorified. But now, in his death and ascent to the Father, Jesus is lifted up to glory. The gift of the Spirit is inseparably linked in John's thought with the death of the One on whom at baptism the Spirit came and remained (1.32 – 33).

Thomas is not present for this encounter between Jesus and the disciples. When later he receives their testimony, 'We have seen the Lord,' Thomas says that he will not believe unless he sees and touches Jesus, risen from the dead. Then, a week later, although the doors are locked, Jesus comes again and stands among them, and challenges Thomas to reach out and touch him. There is a sense of irony in this. Does Thomas really have to touch and prove to himself that it is Jesus? More important than touch, Jesus calls on him to doubt no longer but to believe.

So Thomas makes the confession of faith which is the crown of the Fourth Gospel – 'My Lord and my God!' (verse 28). It is one of the few places in the New Testament where such a close connection between Jesus and God is made.

Most of the readers of John's Gospel, even the earliest, have had no chance of seeing Jesus. John does not say whether Thomas did touch the risen Christ but he does tell us that Thomas **believed**. The point is that those who could have touched him have no advantage over the rest of us. Thomas is representative of the privileged eye-witnesses. Now, by the Spirit who takes of the things of Christ and shows them to us, we may come to know the blessedness of those who have not seen but believe and, in believing, have life in his name.

## Jesus appears in Galilee  John 21.1–14

John 20.30 – 31 reads like the end of the Gospel, giving as it does a clear reason for the writing. This has led some scholars to think of chapter 21 as an appendix, composed by another author. There is no evidence for this in the ancient manuscripts although some words used in this chapter are not found in the rest of this Gospel. Perhaps John used another tradition of stories of the resurrection, those based in Galilee.

This story is set on and by the Sea of Tiberias, also known as Lake Galilee. Seven disciples are present, of which five are named. Peter announces that he is going fishing – that is, going back to work and the others agree to join him. Although the night is the best time for fishing they catch nothing. The story has echoes of Luke 5.1–11. Perhaps John sees the reference to empty nets symbolically – the disciples' mission is fruitless without the presence of the risen Lord.

We are told that just after daybreak Jesus stands on the shore, unrecognised. After learning about the disciples' fruitless night the stranger gives instructions to cast their net on the right side of the boat. There is immediate success. Does John want us to see that this is due to their obedience to the Lord? There is a great haul of fish and the beloved disciple says to Peter, 'It is the

Lord.' Peter makes himself properly clothed and plunges in to reach Jesus and greet him.

Jesus has prepared a meal of fish and bread for the disciples. In early Christian art, fish was often a symbol for the Eucharist. John tells us that the disciples' haul is huge – the net is 'full of large fish' – the kind of catch that prompts amazement and wonder. Yet the net is not torn! Is this to be understood symbolically as John's concern for the unity of the Church? The special mention of one hundred and fifty-three fish probably means something but no one knows for sure what it is.

In their hearts the disciples know, without asking, that it is the Lord. He acts as host, taking bread and giving it to them, and then fish. John says that this is the third time Jesus has appeared to his disciples. The other two times presumably are John 20.19 and 20.26.

## Peter is forgiven and commissioned   John 21.15 – 19

At least twice Jesus and Peter met across a charcoal fire; here at the lakeside (see verse 9) and earlier in the courtyard of the high priest (see John 18.18). On that occasion Peter denied the Lord three times. Now he is confronted by the risen Jesus who calls him not Peter, meaning 'the Rock', but by his old name of Simon. Three times the question is pressed, 'Do you love me?' and three times the affirmation is given; and each time there follows the gracious pastoral charge. Simon is commissioned again.

Behind this story may well be the memory of the Upper Room discussion where Peter promised to follow Jesus, even to lay down his life for him (John 13.36 – 38). With the memory of Jesus' crucifixion Peter now knows what following Jesus will mean for him – it will mean the cross (verse 18b). So the story reaches its climax in the call, 'Follow me' (verse 19).

Peter, with new pastoral responsibility, has learned that to follow Jesus will mean caring for Jesus' disciples in the Lord's own way. It will also mean following him to martyrdom. The resurrection of Jesus means forgiveness and new challenge for Peter.

### The destiny of the beloved disciple   John 21.20 – 23

The beloved disciple is an important figure in the Fourth Gospel. Tradition has it that he is John, the brother of James, one of the twelve, and that he is the author of the Gospel. However, most scholars are not so sure about this, and some go so far as to suggest that the beloved disciple is in fact an ideal character.

Peter, having been recommissioned for pastoral care of the Church asks about the beloved disciple, the one who reclined next to Jesus at the supper. What will happen to him? Will he be martyred too? Jesus' reply has a sharpness about it. Does it matter what others will do in the purposes of God? The individual challenge from the risen Christ to Peter remains, 'Follow me.'

### Some more first reflections

In chapter 5 we shall develop some of the wide-ranging theological implications of these Gospel stories. Here we only hint at two themes to be explored later:

> We have noticed in John's Gospel how the movement to glory – the 'going to the Father' – is

one 'ascension' that begins at the cross. There is often

deep irony in John's writing and it certainly finds expression here. The enemies of Jesus lift him up onto the cross but by so doing they set him on the course to glory. The cross is the place of glory. In doing the Father's will the glory of God is revealed.

So the resurrection in the Fourth Gospel is not in any sense a dramatic divine intervention to get Jesus out of a disastrous hole. Rather it is all of a piece, one movement of ascension from the cross to glory. The resurrection life of Jesus is the fruits of the earlier victory won in the garden and at the cross.

John's way of telling the resurrection story indicates the way in which the raising up of Jesus has implications for others. We shall look at this in more detail later and for the moment we record that the resurrection of Jesus meant Mary moving from the dead end of grief to new hopes and possibilities, Thomas moving from doubt to faith, and Peter from being a failure to beginning a new ministry.

One other feature of John's Gospel that scholars often remark upon is the likelihood that many of its settings are related to the regular Sunday gatherings of the Church, and to the Eucharist or Holy Communion in particular. What is the connection between our worship today and encountering the risen Christ?

### A prayer

Living God, whose Son is the way, the truth and the life, may he so live in us and we in him, that we walk with courage in his way, believe and trust in his truth, and know in our experience his resurrection life. Amen.

**Some questions and suggestions for further thought**

1 What distinctive features do you see in John's account of the resurrection that mark it off from the accounts in the Synoptic Gospels?

2 Think of modern situations that correspond to the experiences of Mary, Thomas and Peter. How can the gospel of resurrection become real for the bereaved, the doubting and those heavy with a sense of failure?

3 What would you say to modern Thomases who declare that they will not believe in the risen Jesus until they see the evidence? Do you know a modern Thomas to whom you could talk about these things?

# 4
# Paul and the resurrection

The Good News of what God has done in Jesus was preached right from the time when the apostles received the Holy Spirit fifty days after Easter (see Acts 2). But the earliest written words we have come from Paul. We turn now to Paul's testimony to the resurrection which comes to us in the form of letters.

Even in the days of the early Church, a letter was different from a sustained piece of reflective theology. Although Paul writes in a profound way, his aim is to address a particular circumstance. He has a picture in his mind of those to whom he is writing, and two things follow from this:

● The first is that we must try, as far as possible, to be aware of the particular conditions and situation of those to whom Paul was writing.

● The second is that we must not expect his thoughts always to be expressed in the same way, nor all of his themes to be orderly and systematic. The letters from Paul are from various backgrounds, journeys, imprisonments, and much else. He was no stuck-at-the-desk scholar but a missionary by divine call and appointment, and his writing and reflection must be seen for what it is. This means that it is difficult to identify Paul's doctrine of the resurrection.

In this chapter we shall look at some of the key passages in Paul's letters where resurrection is the theme. Our intention is not to set forth Paul's thoughts on the resurrection, with all their implications and

53

detail; but rather to 'listen' to him bearing witness as he writes to the different churches and readers. We begin with one of Paul's most well-known chapters.


## The importance of the resurrection   1 Corinthians 15

Paul was the agent, under God, who founded the Christian church in Corinth, sometime between AD 49–51. The town itself was a volatile place, a seaport, with a reputation for rowdiness and immorality. It was also one of those places where there were many religions on offer. All kinds of cults, theories, sects and beliefs were present together with their temples and, sometimes, secret ceremonies. We must not imagine that the whole city responded to Paul's missionary visit in the way that Nineveh turned to God following Jonah's preaching. But a church was certainly planted, and a small group of Christians were established in Corinth.

What we call 1 Corinthians has two sources. First, Paul is responding to things he has heard about the church in Corinth, much of which gives him cause for concern. Secondly, there are issues of faith and morals in which the young church is seeking apostolic guidance. Paul writes in response to their request for help (see, for example, 1 Corinthians 7.1). 1 Corinthians 15 belongs with the first group: in this chapter Paul is concerned with what is being said and believed in Corinth about the resurrection.

It appears that some in Corinth are denying the resurrection of the dead. They may be doing this for several possible reasons – for example, some may be believers in the immortality of the soul but not in the resurrection of the body; or, there may be those who simply do not believe in any kind of life after death except some shadowy unreal state of being. Whatever it is, there is a denial of the resurrection and to this Paul responds.

## What Paul has received   1 Corinthians 15.1–11

Paul is insistent that the message he has proclaimed to the Corinthians was not of his own making but something he had been given. He handed on only what he had 'received' (verse 3). Almost, certainly, Paul is drawing upon a tradition used in preaching in the early Church before his conversion. (The language of 'sins' and 'the twelve' is not common in Paul.) The content of the tradition is that:

● Christ died for our sins in accordance with the Scriptures.
● He was buried.
● He was raised on the third day in accordance wih the Scriptures.
● A list of 'appearances'.

The verb translated 'he was raised' in verse 4 is a strong one, usually denoting an interventive act of God. God raised Jesus to a new state of existence.

We must note straight away that in this early testimony there is no account of the resurrection itself, only of the phenomena, such as the empty tomb and the angels that go with it. In Paul's writing, there are no words of the risen Christ, nor any direct reference to the empty tomb or to the women. This is not to say that Paul did not know of these, or that he did not believe they were necessary. It only means that the tradition of proclaiming the resurrection which he received centred on the appearances.

Paul begins with Cephas (Peter) and then the twelve – possibly relating to Luke 24.34 – 49. Then comes a reference to more than five hundred, some of whom Paul says are alive at the time of writing. It is possible, but not provable, that Paul is here referring to Acts 2 and the day of Pentecost. We are told nothing in the Gospels of the appearance to James (verse 7). But then Paul comes to himself, 'he appeared also to me' (verse 8). What does this word 'appeared' mean? We shall return to that later, but first we shall interrupt our reading of 1 Corinthians and turn to the account of Paul's conversion encounter with the living Christ, given in the Acts of the Apostles.

## Paul's (Saul's) conversion   Acts 9.1–19

This is the first of three accounts of Paul's conversion which are to be found – the other two are in Acts 22.4 – 16 and Acts 26.9 – 18. Paul himself writes about the event in Galatians 1.13 – 17. There he does not describe the Damascus Road incident, but clearly it is very important for the story of the spreading Church in Acts.

Damascus was a significant Jewish centre. Saul (Paul) was going there to do violence to the Christians. He set off in high missionary spirit. There has been consider-able speculation about Saul's own inner attitudes at this time. He had had a strict training in the Torah. He probably possessed a deep longing for greater personal righteousness, so strong that he had already sensed the inadequacy of the Torah to bring him peace. He was present at the martyrdom of Stephen and he also

witnessed the endurance of those Christians against
whom he had already taken action (Acts 8.1–3). But
the story is told in a way which avoids all psychological
probing in the sense that there is no attempt to inquire
into Paul's state of mind concerning the effect of
Stephen's martyrdom on his own thinking. Saul's
conversion is not described as an event internal to
himself, but set out objectively.

Something happens. A voice calls his name, twice, as
Abraham, Jacob and Moses were addressed (see
Genesis 22.11; 46.2; Exodus 3.4). Saul asks who it is
that calls, and he gets the answer, 'I am Jesus, whom
you are persecuting.' The encounter is between Saul
and the risen Christ, Christ who is identified with his
people. To persecute the Church is to persecute Christ
himself.

Saul is struck with blindness and has to be led like a
child. He completes the journey to Damascus and there
meets Ananias. Ananias has been told of Saul's coming
and that he is to respond to him positively because
Christ has called and chosen Saul for important work.
Ananias receives this message, not in an encounter
with the risen Christ, but in a vision – in Acts, a
common means of learning what the disciples are to do.
And so there comes that very dramatic moment when
the enemy turned missionary, the persecutor turned
disciple, is greeted by one who feared him with the
words, 'Brother Saul'. One consequent meaning of
resurrection in this story is that an enemy, even the first
public persecutor of the Church, may yet be transformed into a brother or sister through an encounter
with the risen Christ.

The story in Acts 9, of course, is not just about
conversion but about a vocation. In no sense does the

writer of Acts suggest that this is normative for all Christians. In a particular way Saul has met with Christ. For him it means that he has seen the Lord, and this has taken place by the Lord's initiative. The raising up of Jesus has led to the raising up of Saul.

We now return to Corinthians 15.

## Appearances

Paul's testimony to the resurrection was grounded in his personal experience. Like others, he has met with Christ. Jesus, risen from the dead, has taken the initiative and 'appeared' (1 Corinthians 15.8). The idea of 'appearing' seems to imply the following:

• The risen Christ initiates these events. He is not conjured up by religious or magical means; Christ emerges from his hiddenness beyond our sight.

• Such an appearance is tantamount to revelation. Jesus reveals himself as the crucified but risen One.

• The appearances are moments of challenge. They confront people with a choice. There is no way to avoid this inevitable involvement. For Paul, the fact that he becomes a witness to the resurrection involves the calling to proclaim what once he thought was dangerous blasphemy – that is, that Jesus is the Christ.

• There is a contrast between the language of visions and appearances. Visions or dreams are means through which God might communicate something of his will and calling. The appearances are visually objective events. There is no way we ourselves can get behind this use of different words, but we can note that Paul is not concerned with the psychological or emotional aspects of what happened. For him, he saw the Lord, he heard the Lord call his name and he was made blind for some days.

So, although Paul uses this definite objective language, he understands that resurrection does not mean that an old dead corpse has been resuscitated; but rather that a radical transformation has taken place.

### Christ really is raised   1 Corinthians 15.12 – 34

Paul has just asserted that the resurrection is a historical fact. He 'knows' that Christ is risen – he himself has met the Lord. So how can some in Corinth say there is no resurrection of the dead? If there is no resurrection, then Christ is not raised and the Christian message is false. The question is an urgent one for Paul because he believes that here there is something more at stake than the actual occurrence of an historic fact.

Drawing on his Jewish background, Paul regards our death as inseparably related to our being sinners (Romans 6.23). If then the Corinthians' faith in the God who raised up Jesus from the dead turns out to be false, then the Corinthians and all other believers are in that sinful state that leads to death and death alone. If Christ is not raised then the whole of Christianity is futile. Paul, with the Corinthians, has particularly in mind those who have trusted Christ as Saviour but have already died. He seems to have a strong expectation that Christ would return to earth in glory during his own lifetime. As the years went on and Christ did not return, so Church members died. Were they now utterly lost? Is it for this life only that God has given us hope? That would be the tragic implication of it all if there is no resurrection, as some were saying.

Paul goes on asserting the fact of Christ's resurrection (verse 20). More than that, the resurrection of Christ leads to the resurrection of all those who belong to him. Paul makes this point by drawing a contrast between Adam and Christ. The result of Adam's action was death, a sentence passed on him, and not on him only, but on all humankind – 'all die in Adam' (verse 22). Paul writes out of a strong sense of corporateness. Christ resembles Adam in this respect, namely that what happened to him also has consequences for the whole human race. Where Adam means death, Christ means life as God raises him from the dead.

Paul speaks of Christ in his resurrection as the 'firstfruits' of those who have died (verse 20). Part of what he means here is linked with his thought about the imminent end of the world. The return of Christ, the One whom God raised from the dead, will mean the destruction of everything that stands in challenge and contradiction to the will and love of God. All authorities and powers that contest the lordship of Christ will be overcome. All Christ's enemies will be made subject to him and the last enemy to be destroyed is death. It is important for us to try and grasp the dimensions of Paul's thought here. He sees the great event of Easter as a fundamental turning-point in human history and experience. A preliminary defeat of death has been made but complete victory is yet to come. This is what is meant by the 'eschatological' tension in Paul's thought – the difference between the **now** of Christ's resurrection and the **not yet** of his coming. At the end, when all powers are defeated, Christ will present to the Father a universe where his sovereignty is free and absolute. Christians can live in this hope, even in a world like this, because of the resurrection of Jesus.

### What kind of a body? 1 Corinthians 15.35 – 58

Perhaps in the time of Paul, like today, there were some people who did not believe in the resurrection because of the obvious difficulty in imagining the kind of existence it is. Paul's Jewishness shows in his evident desire to speak of a resurrection body and, to explain what he means, he uses an illustration from the world of nature – the seed and the plant. The seed planted in the soil corresponds to our earthly life and the plant that springs from the seed is resurrection existence. Within the illustration Paul employs the following four ideas:

● Just as we cannot describe in detail what the plant which comes from a seed will be like, so we should not expect to know what resurrection life is like. Indeed, to ask what it will be like is a foolish question. We cannot even begin to guess what our new form will be, but that should not dull our faith in God's ability to create new forms of life. Further, Paul draws attention to the variety of life-forms already in God's creation (verse 39).

● The plant is different from the seed, although it is related to it. So, unlike those Jews who believed in the continuity of our present physical bodies in resurrection, the Corinthians do not have to believe that at all. Indeed, Paul later affirms that 'flesh and blood cannot inherit the kingdom of God' (verse 50). What is perishable will inevitably perish. Resurrection is not the resuscitation of our physical bodies.

● Just as the plant has a beauty and life which the seed does not possess, so the resurrection life will be more glorious than our present existence.

● But there remains some continuity, both between the seed and the plant and between our bodies and the resurrection. We shall be the same people, not entirely different personalities in the resurrection life.

Paul, therefore, speaks of two related but distinct kinds of existence. Our physical bodies are part of this world that is passing away. By contrast, Paul speaks of a spiritual body and it is important that he still speaks of this in body language. He is not advocating belief in disembodied spirits! Again he uses the Adam/Christ contrast. Adam is a life-giving being, belonging to the earth, physical and human; Christ is life-giving, but from heaven. Christ brings into being a new form of human existence, imperishable and eternal.

Then, in verse 50 onwards, Paul reflects on the situation of those Christians in Corinth, like himself, who will be alive when Christ comes. We shall be changed, he says, thinking of the living not the dead. Our earthly body will be transformed from the perishable Adam into the imperishable body of Christ. Death is real, the last enemy, and Paul pictures it like a scorpion's sting – but thanks be to God for the victory won over sin and death.

So confident is Paul that he concludes the chapter by urging the Christians at Corinth to go on with their work, excelling in it, because in Christ nothing of that will ever be lost.

## Some other verses from Paul

We have concentrated our attention on 1 Corinthians 15 because it is the most direct of Paul's writings on the theme of resurrection. In fact, whether in Corinth, Jerusalem, Ephesus or Philippi, Paul's thoughts and actions were never far away from that moment on the

Damascus Road when he encountered the risen Jesus.
This was decisive. It put the whole of his life in a new
context and set him off in a direction, with a task he
could never have imagined. As he said, 'I have seen the
Lord.'

So, there is a sense in which all Paul's writings are
shot through with resurrection. It is the foundation of
everything he has to say. He does not give us any
further reflection on appearances of the Lord, neither
does he refer to the empty tomb – although he does
assert the full humanity of Jesus. His constant reference
is to the new life in Christ. As an illustration of that we
shall look briefly at verses from three more of his
letters.

### Baptism and resurrection   Romans 6.1–11

These verses are part of Paul's great argument on the
theme of God's justification of sinners. By his gracious
work, God sets us free from sin and its results. Any
who think that they can take God and his grace for
granted have gravely misunderstood the gospel and, in
particular, the significance of the death of Jesus. Paul
illustrates his argument with reference to baptism.

He understands baptism as being 'into Christ Jesus'.
Christians were baptised in the name of Jesus Christ
(see Acts 2.38 and 8.12). To be baptised into Christ
implied initiation into the body of Christ, the Church.
But Paul also has in his mind the theme of a new
humanity, no longer under the power of sin and death,
and no longer living by ancient divisions and
distinctions (Galatians 3.28), but a new existence.

This is baptism into the death of Christ (verse 3). In

baptism we are buried with Christ (verse 4). Our old self is laid in the tomb with Jesus. Paul can even speak of being crucified with Christ (Galatians 2.19). The references to the resurrection in these verses from Romans all point forward to the future. Baptism proclaims the dying and rising, but the new resurrection order has yet to come fully. Even so, by baptism into Christ Jesus, the believer lives in the realm where God is sovereign. It is the realm where death no longer rules (verse 9). Paul can assert that, because of the resurrection of Jesus, believers may live also. Death no longer has dominion.

## New creation   2 Corinthians 5.17

Again we encounter the emphasis on something new happening in history through what God has accomplished in the life, death and resurrection of Jesus. Paul is not talking about an individual experience like being 'born again'. He is proclaiming a new work of creation, a new humanity, a new existence in Christ Jesus. The old order, in Adam, is not the last word. That word is with God who, in Christ, has turned over the catastrophic results of Adam's sin. The old has passed away; the new creation is here in Christ. It is all the work of God, reconciling the world to himself. Paul, and the whole Church, is given the task of announcing this good news of new life.

## To know the risen Christ more
   Philippians 1.21–26; 2.5–11; 3.10

In the letter to the Philippians there are three extracts in particular which illustrate the significance of the resurrection of Jesus for Paul's life.

● **Philippians 1.21–26.** In a series of parallel statements Paul sets out the reality of life for him after his encounter with the risen Christ on the Damascus Road. He can hardly put it more sharply. To live is Christ, even though there may be many risks and hardships in being an apostle. He writes from a prison cell but he believes that, in Christ, he shares God's new creation. Thus, even if he were to die it will be a gain, in two senses: one, he will go to be with Christ, to a deeper fellowship with the Lord; two, his own martyrdom will proclaim Christ and bring fruit.

● **Philippians 2.5–11.** It has been suggested that here Paul is quoting a hymn used in the early Church. These verses tell of the humble obedience of Jesus, even to death on the cross. But Paul's gospel is solidly proclaimed in the affirmation that it is this crucified Jesus whom God has exalted above all other names. God has made him Lord. The resurrection is of massive significance.

● **Philippians 3.10.** Paul rejoices in knowing Christ Jesus as Lord. Here he expresses his great longing. It is to know Christ more – in his resurrection power, as in the living encounter on the Damascus Road, and in sharing his sufferings, as in the privilege of ministry, the costly road of discipleship in and with Christ.

### Some concluding reflections

Paul gives us no detail of the historic resurrection of Jesus – he simply proclaims that as a fact. He gives us no references to the empty tomb and the events of

Easter Day. Rather he simply proclaims, on the basis of his experience, that Christ is risen. We have seen how fundamental and basic that is for Paul's whole understanding of the gospel. We can summarise this in three ways:

Paul sees in the resurrection of Christ Jesus the ground of new life for humankind. He draws a sharp contrast between Adam and Christ. There is an existence that leads only to death and there is the new life in Christ. Jesus shared our sinful world and its consequential death; but God raised him and the cycle of sin and deadly despair is broken. A new humanity is brought into being and we share it by God's gracious gift of faith in Christ. By baptism we are united with him. This new humanity is different from the old. Its membership does not rest on nationality, economic status or sex – there is neither Jew nor Greek, slave nor free, male nor female. In and through Christ, God is creating a new humanity.

Paul, therefore, sees the resurrection of Jesus Christ as a great cause for hope. It is important for us to grasp the tension in his thought. Christ has been raised from the dead and a victory is won. But Paul speaks of Christ's resurrection as 'first-fruits'; the completed resurrection is still to come. This eschatological element in Paul must not be overlooked. Resurrection belongs to the end, the completed purposes of God. The raising up of Jesus therefore is a taste of the real thing, for the One who will come at the end is this Christ. That is the Christian hope.

So we live 'in between'. We are called to live the new life in Christ and Paul is aware, not least in his own experience, that that means costly sacrificial discipleship. However, that is as nothing compared with knowing Christ. It can hardly be called a sacrifice at all. But the two things go together – life in Christ, hopeful and joyful, and suffering with and for Christ. The resurrection of Jesus does not mean the end of pain, struggle, suffering and sorrow in this life but, in the midst of it all, we are not broken. We need never lose heart. We may be beaten down, crushed, greatly troubled and much else but that is not the whole story by any means (see 2 Corinthians 6.1–10). In a dark world we have glimpsed the light of God in the face of Jesus Christ. So, even though we suffer, we shall not give up. If we are like Paul, we shall even rejoice!

## A prayer

Living Lord, in whose sacrifice we know forgiveness, in whose resurrection we are given hope, in whose will is our peace, grant us grace to live the life in Christ, resisting evil, overcoming cruel divisions, and rejoicing in the gift of new creation, through Jesus Christ our Lord. Amen.

## Some questions and suggestions for further thought

1  Think of ways in which the local church can witness to the new humanity in Christ. What divisions in our churches, or in the wider communities in which we live, do we recognise as standing in challenge to the new creation God offers us in Christ?

2 What would you say to a congregation, a minister, or a church member who has lost heart as a Christian? (2 Corinthians 4 might be a helpful place to begin your reflection.)

3 Where do you see today's Church sharing in Christ's sufferings? And where do you see local congregations living as signs of hope?

4 Not all conversions are as dramatic as Paul's. Find out how some other people became Christians.

# 5
# Believing in the resurrection

In chapters 2, 3, and 4 we have looked at the main New Testament verses which are concerned with the resurrection of Jesus. We have not been able to deal with all the important texts as there are so many; in fact, the whole of the New Testament is permeated with the message of resurrection. All the New Testament writers believe that they have witnessed God's great work of salvation in the life, death and resurrection of Jesus. They are intent on telling the story of Jesus and drawing out the implications of who he is and what he has done.

Jesus is no dead hero, no noble martyr, worthy to be followed as a moral example. He is Lord, the One whom God has raised from the dead, and the whole of the New Testament affirms this. Our attention to some particular verses should not blind us to the fact that the earliest Christians believed that something crucially new had happened so that everything in life and death had to be looked at afresh.

In chapter 1 we acknowledged that the resurrection of Jesus is problematic in several senses. It is something that appears to be incredible – outside our normal expectations and experience. Its very strangeness is a problem to us. We cannot help but ask if it actually happened. Now in this chapter we shall look again at some of those questions of history, but first let us consider why history is important.

## The importance of history

History has to be taken seriously by Christians. The hard questions of historical events have to be faced precisely because Christianity is an historical religion. The God whom Christians believe in is One who is said to work out his purposes in history – indeed One who entered into history in the full form and experience of human life (see John 1.14).

Christianity, as a religion, is not a theory about life, and certainly not about life after death. There have been religions that draw a clear distinction between body and soul but Christianity has not been among them. It is true that there is some evidence of the influence of the essentially Greek idea of the immortality of the soul in the New Testament but fundamentally it is in terms of Jewish background belief that Christians have spoken about life after death – that is, of the resurrection of the body. And they have spoken in this way because of the resurrection of Jesus.

Jesus was a real figure in history. Things happened to him as they happen to us all. When he went without food, he was hungry; when a close and dear friend died, he wept; when his body was cut open, he bled. Christians believe that this Jesus was raised by God from death. Resurrection is something that happened to this real person – and what happened to him had a real effect on other people. The questions of history, of what happened, may be challenging and difficult but they cannot be avoided by a faith that is historical.

## The existence of the Church

Some people have tried to avoid the most pressing of

the questions of historical fact by arguing that the very existence of the Christian Church proves that Jesus was raised from the dead. After all, so the argument goes, people have died for this conviction and they would not have done so if it were a lie. There have been massive attempts to wipe out the Church, but again and again it flourishes beyond all human expectations. Just when its persecutors, at various times in history, have finally thought that they had wiped out the Church, it reappears vigorously and courageously telling the story of the cross and the empty tomb. It seems indeed that the gates of hell (Hades) cannot prevail against it (see Matthew 16.18). People may doubt the stories of the resurrection of Jesus but no one can seriously question the existence of the Christian Church.

There is obvious force in this argument, and the existence of the Church as an historical phenomenon certainly needs to be explained. There always have been those who have lived and died for Jesus' sake. The noble army of martyrs cannot be ignored; but in themselves they do not amount to proof of the resurrection. The fact of the Church only proves that there has been a continuous stream of men and women throughout history who have believed in the God who raised Jesus from the dead. There would be nothing self-contradictory in saying that all these may have been deluded. However, that such a large number of people, some of whom were ready to die for their faith, were deluded may be more difficult to believe than that their message is true.

Nevertheless, it still does not follow, logically, that Jesus was raised from the dead. There is no way of avoiding the difficult historical question of whether anything did happen to the body of Jesus other than that it decayed as mortal remains somewhere in Palestine.

As we have seen it is the witness of the New Testament that **God** raised Jesus from the dead. Resurrection is an act of God; and, as such, it is beyond proof. We may say that an event happened – even have very good evidence that it happened – but to prove that God caused it to happen is not possible. Resurrection, as the work of God, can only relate to faith, not to proof.

Let us now go back and recall some aspects of the apostles' testimony and the form that their proclamation took.

## The appearances

We saw that an early tradition of witness to the resurrection of Jesus concentrated on the appearances of the risen Christ. This was Paul's testimony in 1 Corinthians 15. Scholars argue about whether Paul knew the tradition of the empty tomb or not, but there is no doubting his own claims to have seen the Lord.

All the appearances of the risen Christ which are recorded in the Gospels were to those who were his disciples. They may not have believed the empty tomb story, as was the case with the two on the road to Emmaus, but they became believers in the risen Lord because of his appearance to them.

It is important that we recall again the way in which these appearance stories are told so as to stress the objectivity of the risen Christ. It was not a ghost which encountered the disciples, nor was this simply something imagined, subjective, internal to the disciples' minds. The stories are told, underlining the unexpectedness of it all and the disciples' lack of faith until Jesus, risen from the dead, encounters them. As the story of the Church shows, the disciples' belief certainly changed them.

Now again, we can deny this and say that it is all in the imagination and wistful thinking of disappointed followers. However, we have to recognise that the way in which they tell the story implies not that the longing of the disciples produced faith in the risen Christ but that the unexpected risen Christ produced faith in the disciples.

### The empty tomb

This, too, we have seen, is a feature of an early tradition of apostolic testimony. On the first Easter Sunday morning the women found that the tomb was empty. The very fact that the women are identified as the primary witnesses may, in an inverted sense, be significant in indicating the authenticity of the story. As we noted in chapter 2, women were not taken seriously as witnesses at that time. It would have been tempting for anyone who was creating a story to have had a man, such as Peter or John, as the first witness, but it was not like that. Mary Magdalene is consistently the one who finds the tomb empty.

There is no description of the resurrection itself. This is in contrast to the apocryphal Gospels, written later in the second century, which became very fanciful at times. What the women find is that the tomb is empty. All kinds of literary means are used to affirm that the body is not there. Perhaps that insistence itself owes much to a Jewish background belief in the resurrection of the body. It is also a consistent feature of the empty tomb stories that no one expected to find anything other than the body of Jesus.

Again we must recognise the logical gap between the empty tomb and the resurrection of Jesus. No one seems to have doubted that the tomb was empty. Matthew recorded a rumour, which he attributes to the Jews, that the disciples had come and stolen the body away. That would account for the empty tomb. There might be other ways of explaining the phenomenon, but the New Testament witness is that Jesus has been raised by God. That is why the tomb is empty.

## What happened?

Once more we ask the question, 'What happened?' (see chapter 1). Because it is an act of God that is being affirmed, we cannot say descriptively what happened. Historically all we can claim is that within three days of his death some of the friends of Jesus were proclaiming that the tomb was empty and that the risen Jesus had actually appeared to them. That is the testimony we have from the apostles as recorded in the New Testament.

Are such stories true? Our answer to that question will depend on the presuppositions we bring with us. Some people will believe that the stories are true, as they stand, on authority. For some, this will be the authority that goes with a particular way of reading the Bible – if it says in the Bible that it happened, then it happened and just in that way. Others will believe the stories on the authority of the teaching church. This can take Protestant as well as Catholic and Orthodox forms. Then there are others who will find it impossible to give over their minds unquestioningly to such authority. They will be puzzled, perhaps frustrated, by the questions of history. They will have to say that they do not know what happened. The historical question cannot be settled, but they do believe in Jesus, risen from the dead, raised by God from the grave to glory.

No one is in a position to say what happened. Even the earliest stories are not wholly consistent in what they say. But we do have testimony – and it is the testimony of those who clearly believed that God had acted in raising up Jesus. These people faced persecution, abuse, poverty and death in this conviction. They described what they believed in letter and narrative form with the concepts and images of their day. Part of what it is to be a Christian is to believe their testimony.

**An eschatological perspective on resurrection**

A number of scholars, noting that no one can really say what happened in the resurrection of Jesus, ask whether we ought to think of it primarily in historical terms at all. Clearly something happened in history – and certainly the long tradition of the witnessing Church is a fact of history, but is the resurrection of Jesus chiefly an event in history?

What these scholars have in mind is the eschatological aspect of the Christian faith. Eschatology is the word scholars use when they speak about the 'last things' – the culmination of all God's purposes. Christians believe that this world is God's creation. Its existence is no accident and, although at times it can appear to be very disordered, shapeless and chaotic, in fact God remains God and his purposes will be brought to completion.

The theme of 'last things' often appears in the Advent season and has to do with death, judgement and the coming of God at the end of history. In Jewish thinking the resurrection of the dead belonged to the 'last things'. We have an echo of that in John's Gospel when Martha confesses her faith that Lazarus will be raised on the last day (see John 11.24).

Taking this approach we could say then that God's raising up of Jesus is an event 'before its time'. It belongs to the end and as such belongs to the completion of all God's purposes beyond space and time. But it has 'broken into' the world's history, and so **the resurrection of Jesus is an event of the future that has happened now**. The New Testament writers express this in different ways.

Paul, for example, sees the raising up of Jesus as the crucial feature of a new age, a new humanity that God is bringing into being where humankind is no longer in slavery to sin and death. The resurrection of Jesus is a promise, a foretaste, a first-fruit, of what will come to fulfilment later. The Christian Church now, in the midst of a sometimes painful and ambiguous history, is nevertheless filled with hope because of the resurrection of Jesus from the dead.

Again, in John's Gospel, when the early Church was beginning to qualify its belief that the end would come quickly, probably in the first apostles' lifetime, the significance of what God had done linked both past, present and future. For example, John's community realised that what had happened in Jesus was what was believed to belong only to the end time. It was not that the Church ceased to believe in the completion of all God's purposes but that the key to these purposes and their fulfilment was found in what God had done in Jesus. So Jesus is not one who will be the resurrection and the life – he is that **now** (see John 11.25). Judgement will not only happen sometime in the future, it is already taking place in Jesus (see John 12.31). Nor is it the case that at some future date and state we shall enter into the life eternal; rather, through Christ that is ours already (see John 6.54, where present and future are united in one text).

When the early Church spoke of the end they centred on Jesus, raised by God. Jesus Christ will come again, bearing the scars from the crucifixion. His resurrection means more than his personal victory for it proclaims the triumph of God's purposes and loving ways.

### The uniqueness of it all

Something happened in human history which Christians call the resurrection of Jesus. Fearful, unbelieving, disappointed disciples came to have courage, faith and hope. They proclaimed that the tomb of the crucified One was empty. They told how Christ had come to them – they had seen the Lord. The event is surprising, disturbing, enlivening and unique.

But how unique? If something is literally totally unique how would we ever recognise it or understand it for what it is? Something totally unique hardly corresponds to our own experience. As such it is in danger of being irrelevant. What could anything so strange have to do with us?

77

Clearly, the New Testament witnesses gave their testimony because they believe that, however remarkable and unique the event might be, it had everything to do with us. In the New Testament letters and Gospels we have hints about how the resurrection of Jesus is important for us and all humankind. The event may be unique but is not totally outside our experience.

We have to remember that the gospel message which the evangelists proclaimed was that God raised Jesus from the dead. This is not a story of a superman leaping up from the grave. It is the work of God – God, whom Jesus called *Abba*, the God of Abraham, Isaac and Jacob, of Sarah, Rachel and Ruth, the God of Israel. This God brought his people out of slavery. He went with them into the humiliation of exile and then brought them back from seemingly despair and defeat to new beginnings. This is the God who raised Jesus from the dead, the God whose kingdom is being proclaimed in the life, death and resurrection of Jesus.

The God of Israel is known in Jesus Christ. From this basis we can begin to see where this God is at work today. The final two chapters of John's Gospel give us clues. For example, there is the story of **Mary** who comes to the tomb, broken-hearted in her grief. She knows the anger that goes with bereavement. Her tears distort her vision. Here is a picture of a woman of deep love plunged into the darkness of the valley of the shadow of death. What is there to live for? Who cares? What value does her own life have now? And then comes the calling of her name. She is known and valued. The love she counted on so much has not let her go. In this encounter the resurrection of Jesus is Mary's resurrection also. God again lifts up the fallen and heals the broken-hearted. Wherever there is the kind of loving pastoral friendship that helps people in their grief, calls them by name and strengthens them to enter into the future, there is the living power of God that raised Jesus from the dead.

Also there is **Thomas**. He cannot believe the story his friends tell. Thomas is a sensible man with his feet on the ground. He needs evidence before he will accept what is way beyond his experience. Why cannot people bear the reality of life, cold and hard as it is, without these flights into wishful thinking that lead inevitably to disappointment? Thomas is not a wicked man. He was devoted to Jesus. He was the one who stuck by the Lord when he wanted to go to the tomb of Lazarus (see John 11.16). Doubtless Thomas was disappointed at the result of Jesus' ministry but he would not escape that by believing a fancy. And then the risen Lord comes to meet him. The experience is undeniable. He is not argued out of his doubt but confronted by a presence, and proclaims, 'My Lord and my God!' (John 20.28). Resurrection happens when Thomas – or anyone else – is led from unquestioning doubt to personal faith. 'Blessed are those who have not seen and yet have come to believe' (John 20.29).

And then there is **Peter**. He had promised that, although all others failed, he would never deny the Lord, but the unthinkable happened. Before the questioning of a woman (girl) and a slave (servant) he failed (see John 18.17, 26–27) – and the Lord knew it! How could Peter ever lift up his head again? He would carry that grief with him for always. And then one morning, he is taken aside and asked, 'Do you love me?' Three times the question is asked, each one more painful than the last. But it had to be three – remember the three denials! And through it all there was given to

Peter a ministry, an assurance and a realisation that his failure was not the last word about his life. His failure was forgiven. More than that, he who had failed was entrusted once more with ministry, the Lord's ministry to the Lord's people. Resurrection happens wherever failures are forgiven, when a future that seems closed for ever is opened again with trust, and the gift of new responsibility is offered. Jesus' resurrection made possible the raising up of fallen Peter.

Some of our failures haunt us all our days. A cloud is cast over our life that no breeze seems capable of blowing away. We try to put it out of our mind, and succeed for a while, only to find that our confidence has been shaken deeply.

And so we could go on. Think, for instance, of the meaning of the resurrection of Jesus in the life of the Pharisee, Saul. He received more than a new name, Paul. The point is that the God of resurrection is always present wherever the broken are healed, the fallen are raised up, the despairing are given hope, and sacrifice and love lead to life.

Think of situations you know for yourself. Recently friends have told me of the Christian Church in El Salvador, facing various forms of oppression, knowing mistrust, misrepresentation and persecution, but going on bearing a costly witness to Jesus the Lord. I think of Terry Waite and others who have been held hostage for long periods and have come out from their devastating experience with a deeper commitment to seek justice **and** without bitterness. I think of people like a friend of mine whose body is being wasted by multiple sclerosis but who speak of being given grace, as Paul did, enough grace for each day so that the life of Christ shines in their lives. All these, and many more, are witness to the resurrection. The raising of Jesus by God is indeed a unique event in human history but what it means is not totally outside our experience, thank God!

## Resurrection mission

One feature of the resurrection stories recorded in the Gospels is the relation between an appearance of the risen Jesus to the disciples and the calling to mission. This is most evident in John's Gospel where Jesus, sent by the Father, now sends the apostles (see John 20.21).

Paul understood that the appearance of Christ Jesus to him on the Damascus Road was primarily for a missionary purpose. His confrontation by Christ, alive by the power of God, was his calling to be an apostle, a witness to the resurrection, especially to the Gentiles.

The Church now does not just live with the missionary calling as an inheritance of history; for to believe in the resurrection, to celebrate the Easter faith, is to bear witness, to spread this gospel, and to be part of the mission of the Christlike God. Mission is not therefore something extra to the faith of the Church, for those who like that kind of thing; it goes with the very heart of the matter – the raising up of the Lord Jesus Christ.

## Christ present with his Church

Another feature of the Gospel narratives of the resurrection is that of Christ coming to the disciples as they meet together. It is a theme reflected in other parts of the New Testament and one that is echoed in the experience of the Church – 'Where two or three are

gathered in my name, I am there among them'
(Matthew 18.20).

Here we touch on one other aspect of our Christian
life and experience which relates directly to the
resurrection – Christ present in his Church. There have
been many theologies and understandings of the
Lord's Supper, or Holy Communion, but all of them
affirm the presence of Christ among his people. The
same is true of baptism. The act of baptism is a kind of
focal point, a meeting-place between Christ and not
just the individual but the Church. We may think of
Christ as being present in different ways but none of us
thinks he is absent.

Many Christians tell of moments of awareness when,
for them, the living Christ was powerfully present. It
may have been while they were at prayer, or reading
the Bible, or in the formal worship of the Church.
Whatever it was, Christians speak of an encounter
which, for them, is real and not of their own making.

I myself recall one such moment. It was in 1967. I was
part of one of the first parties to go to the Holy Land
after the Arab/Israeli war. It was a mixed experience,
visiting the biblical sites, reading the Bible stories, and
reflecting on the presence and teaching of Jesus, mostly
with armed soldiers looking on and checking our
movements. Early one Sunday morning, a small group
of us went down to the garden tomb area in Jerusalem.
There we offered our worship of praise and prayer, we
listened to Scripture and in the simplest of ways, in
bread and wine, we celebrated communion. All I can
say is that, for me, it was an utterly overwhelming
experience. I was sure beyond all argument, that Christ
was alive and present with us. Of course the context
added something but the experience was beyond

anything I have known before or since. My faith and calling were renewed within me. It was a moment of glory and grace – a resurrection moment beyond words.

## Jesus Christ the Lord

One last aspect of the resurrection for us to consider is what it means for our discipleship. Peter, in his Pentecostal Sunday sermon, proclaims that God has made this Jesus whom you crucified both Lord and Messiah (from Acts 2.36). The raising up of Jesus by God has massive moral consequences. This is the One over whom God has pronounced his great 'Yes'. It is not Pilate nor Caiaphas nor any other of the great ones who is so acknowledged by God. It is Jesus!

It is Jesus of the towel and basin who washed the disciples' feet, like a common servant. It is Jesus who actively mixed and ate with undesirables and those rejected by society. It is Jesus, who took risks and touched the sick and unclean. It is Jesus who taught that greatness is found in service; and that children, those with no status, are first in the kingdom of heaven. It is Jesus who burst the bubble of pompous religiosity. It is Jesus who would not retaliate. It is Jesus, of the scourging, the humiliation, the crucifixion and the prayer for enemies. It is over this life, this man, despised and rejected, denied and crucified, weak and utterly vulnerable, that God spoke the great 'Amen'. It is this Jesus whom God raised. It is this Jesus who is Lord!

So, to believe in the resurrection in any meaningful way at all is to follow Jesus Christ, to obey him, not

83

simply to call him 'Lord, Lord', but to do what he tells us. For Jesus, raised by God, is the pattern for our Christian life. As the risen One, he is the means by which we receive the promised Holy Spirit to strengthen, lead and encourage us. But he is Lord, and being a Christian means following him, walking in his way, and loving as he loved us.

## A prayer

Living God, always making new,
The resurrection of Jesus challenges us.
We admit, Thomas-like, we find it hard to believe.
It's not that we don't want to!
We **do**! We **do**!
But it is all so amazing –
can it really be true?
Thank you for all those who have believed,
trusted, obeyed, given their lives.
Thank you for your Church,
bearer of the message,
borne by the message.
We cannot push aside this great cloud
    of witnesses.
Your resurrection challenges us
in the lives of saints today –
Mother Teresa, Martin Luther King, Terry Waite –
but not those only.
There are others, we know them,
and in the knowing
cannot deny how their lives glow with your light.
Your resurrection challenges us
to trust, to have faith, to follow;

for, if Christ is risen indeed,
then the world is changed.
We can hope.
We can give ourselves to you.
We can be confident of your love,
in hospital, at the grave, in prison,
in the moment of darkness,
in loneliness, in pain,
we can remember Christ is risen,
and there is nothing at all to separate us
   from your love.

Come, Lord Jesus, live in us.
Come, Lord, we believe, at least a little,
help us to believe even more.
Come, Lord, and live in us,
our home,
our Church,
our world.
And help us to live in you the new life,
resurrection life,
your life, in us.

**Some questions and suggestions for further thought**

1  What do you think are the most important practical
   implications of the resurrection of Jesus for our life
   today?

2  What are the most serious difficulties to be faced in
   believing in the resurrection? How do you think they
   can be met?

3 Ask some other Christians to tell you why they believe in the resurrection of Jesus. Have they any special experiences to share?

4 How would you express your faith in the risen Jesus to a non-believer who asked you about the meaning of Easter?

# 6

# Looking at ascension

Ascension is there in the great Christian creeds. It is there in Scripture. But, in some churches today, it could well be described as the neglected festival. This could be because, apart from Luke, the Gospel writers tend to run resurrection and ascension into one. That is certainly the way in John's Gospel. But, from the early days of the Church, ascension was celebrated as a separate festival.

We can be glad of that and particularly grateful to Luke. There is so much in the good news of resurrection that it is fitting that we can space it out after Easter, examining Sunday by Sunday the story of the raising up of Jesus until it comes to the moment of ascension and we can then hear that message in its own right. It completes the great work of God in Jesus Christ before the pouring out of the Holy Spirit at Pentecost.

Like the accounts of the resurrection in the Gospels we have two kinds of problems with the ascension narratives. One is that they are different in the various Gospels. Luke has the ascension as a distinct event. He ends his Gospel with it and then repeats it as he begins the Acts of the Apostles. John has a different approach. There is no point in trying to harmonise these, let alone reduce them to one form. It is best to let the Gospel writers each speak in their own chosen way so that we hear the full message.

Then, also, as there are historical questions

associated with the resurrection so there certainly are with ascension. The story is set in the thought forms and world view of the first century – we are on earth, heaven is above us and hell below. Some years ago a Russian cosmonaut returned from his flight into space and reported that he had not seen God! Most Christians in the twentieth century century find that a silly comment. But what then are we to make of the ascension story? Where the emphasis in the Gospels has been on 'bodily' resurrection then something must happen to that body. So those who emphasise the historical nature of the resurrection do so with the ascension. Others deny that the ascension is an event in space and time; they interpret it differently.

We shall not enter into that debate. Our priority in this chapter will be to look at some key Bible verses. We shall do this by concentrating on the Scripture readings for Ascension Day and the Sunday after Ascension in the most widely-used lectionaries in Britain, adding some verses from John. Only then shall we reflect on the theological richness of this aspect of our faith summed up in the phrase, 'He ascended into heaven.'

## The ascension of Elijah    2 Kings 2.1–15

This is a marvellously dramatic picture whose meaning is not obviously clear. In fact it has several meanings. It is both about the departure of Elijah and the commissioning of Elisha.

Elijah is taken up to heaven in a whirlwind. Devastating dust storms are not unknown in that part of the world. They represent great power and energy.

However, in the Old Testament, the Hebrew word for wind – *ruach* – is the same as that for spirit, and so perhaps something more than a natural phenomenon is implied from the start.

Companies of professional prophets, with whom Elijah had often stood in opposition as they supported the policies of the kings, prophesy his departure. Elisha does not do as he is commanded but stays with his master. Elijah strikes the waters of the Jordan so that they part and the two cross to the other side. We are here reminded of Moses; this is the tradition in which Elijah stands.

The end is coming near, so Elijah asks Elisha what he can do for him. When Elisha asks for a 'double share' (verse 9) of the prophet's spirit his request is to receive as if he were the eldest son (Deuteronomy 21.17). But only God can give such a gift if he wills.

Then Elisha and Elijah are separated by a chariot and horses of fire, and Elijah ascends in the whirlwind into heaven. It is by no means clear what is being described here. Chariots in Israel would have reminded the people of at least two things. The Canaanites used chariots when they fought against their enemies, but the Israelites had no chariots. Also a feature of Canaanite worship was of the sun-god in his chariot. Israel rejected this, of course, but they did not discard the symbol. It appears in Psalm 68.17 and Habakkuk 3.8 where the Lord's chariots and horses are mentioned. So, although God does not appear in the ascension of Elijah, the chariot and horsemen may well represent the power of God.

The rest of this passage is then concerned with the commission of Elisha. But, according to later traditions in both Judaism and Christianity, Elijah's ministry does

word of Jesus. As such they are models for the Christian life. As disciples they share the power of the risen Lord, and they are called to pass on his teaching faithfully.

Another feature of Matthew's Gospel is the importance of 'the mountain'. It is there in the temptation and transfiguration stories (see Matthew 4.8 and 17.1). The great teaching sermon is given on a mountain (Matthew 5.1). The reference to the mountain alerts to the possibility of a significant event about to happen.

We ought also to note the reference to Galilee. Matthew's is the most Jewish of the four Gospels. Galilee was a neglected part of Israel, with a huge percentage of Gentiles in the population. It was the territory in which Jesus was forced to live his early days (Matthew 2.22). Is Matthew suggesting here that the good news of the gospel cannot stay in Jerusalem, in Israel, but that it must go out from Galilee, into the Gentile world?

Jesus comes to the eleven and the response is one of worship, although some doubted. We cannot tell whether these are some of the eleven or some other disciples. We have recognised in this book that there is something totally awe-inspiring yet unbelievable in the whole idea of resurrection. Matthew is recognising this. It is not direct disbelief that is identified here but understandable doubt. Such doubt is overcome not by dogmatic argument but by hearing the gospel word and obeying it. Resurrection faith always requires the active decision of trust.

Jesus declares that authority in heaven and on earth has been given to him. There is an echo here of the verses we have just looked at in Daniel 7, especially verse 14. In the Septuagint, the Greek translation of the Old Testament, this verse is very close to the language of Matthew 28.18. What it means is that Jesus is the direct and human expression of the will of God. The risen Jesus, whose authority is so far-reaching, is the teacher and judge who belongs to the completion of all God's purposes, the eschatological prophet.

And what he says is, 'Go . . . make disciples', not just among the people of Israel, but from all nations. The mission of God is to **all**. We note the 'therefore' in verse 19. It is because all authority is with Jesus that, **therefore**, the disciples must go and make disciples. Baptism was the mark of becoming a Christian and, whereas in other parts of the New Testament baptism is in the name of Jesus, here it is to be in the full name of God: the Father, the Son and the Holy Spirit. With baptism goes teaching, all the stories and commands of Jesus. The apostles are to help new disciples to understand and obey and so walk the way of life that is under the authority of Jesus.

These verses end with a great promise. Jesus is not with his friends as he was before. There is no body for them to literally touch and see; but there is his presence, promised to the end of the age. When he first came he was named *Immanuel* – God with us. So it was, is and will be. The humanity Jesus shared, through which the gracious presence of God was known, is now taken into heaven, into the presence of God. This Jesus has authority everywhere. He is everywhere with his people.

## A first look at ascension   Luke 24.44 – 53

These closing verses of Luke's Gospel are full of

recalls the appearances of the risen Christ, not as vision, but as real encounters. In contrast to the Gospel he speaks of this taking place over forty days. Only Luke among the Gospel writers suggests this chronology. 'Forty days' is a time often mentioned in Scripture for a period of intense spiritual concentration and significance. Luke gives us the picture of the risen Jesus with the disciples, teaching and instructing them on the theme of the kingdom of God so that their understanding of his mission is deepened.

The apostles are in Jerusalem, as they had been bidden by Christ. The Father has a promise to fulfil but the Holy Spirit cannot be given until Jesus has ascended.

The question in verse 6 about the restoration of the kingdom to Israel is, on the face of it, strange, given that the apostles have had many days of instruction. There were current hopes in Israel that God would bring about a triumphant work of liberation from the oppressive Romans, Jesus replies that the times are God's business (see the reference in Mark 13.32); but he also reiterates the promise, speaking, as is consistent in Luke and Acts, of the Holy Spirit in terms of power.

Then, suddenly, with the word of promise scarcely finished, Jesus is lifted up. The phrase affirms the apostolic conviction that Jesus has been raised to glory, to the right hand of God, to the place of authority. Luke does not say that he disappeared into the clouds, as we might lose sight of an aeroplane. He says that a cloud took him out of their sight. Often in the Bible the cloud is a symbol of the mystery of God's presence. It is into this that Christ is received.

The two men in white robes appear (see Luke 24.4). They have a message and basically it is that the disciples must now be prepared to start their work. There is no point in gazing up into the sky, no point in looking longingly for Jesus. There is the promise of the return of Jesus, the same Jesus who was once known in the flesh but who now reigns in glory.

If the ascension at the close of the Gospel marked the conclusion of Jesus' earthly ministry, now the ascension at the beginning of Acts marks the start of the ministry of the Church.

### Going to the Father   John 16.1–11

We saw in chapter 3 of this book how John sees Jesus' journey from the cross, to the grave, to resurrection, to exaltation and glory as one single episode. Although that is in contrast to the way Luke tells his Gospel story, essentially the Gospel writers are saying the same thing.

The setting of John 16.1–11 is the Upper Room. Jesus is pictured as sharing many things with his disciples. Our reading opens with the theme of coming persecution. Jesus warns the disciples that this will happen to them. They already know that it has happened to him – and the cross is still to come. The warning is that a time will come when Jewish Christians will be put out of the synagogues, no longer able to share the worship. The terrible irony in this is that those who shut them out do so in the conviction that they are giving honour to God. Many think that John's Gospel was written at a time when this had already begun to happen. Jesus is pictured here as telling the disciples of this so that his words will be remembered when it happens.

Jesus openly tells them that the hour for his departure is coming nearer. He has taught his disciples the truth but now his impending departure adds urgency. He must prepare them. The sorrow of the disciples shows that they are more concerned with their own grief than with the thought of losing Jesus. They do not understand what is going on.

Jesus affirms that it is for their good that he is going. If he does not go, the Spirit will not be given. The positive thrust in the message is in the phrases, 'If I go, I will send him to you' (verse 7). The disciples must be helped to accept his going in a positive frame of mind so that they are ready and capable of receiving the Spirit. The ascension of Jesus is seen here as positively part of the Gospel, an essential element in God's purposes.

The remainder of these verses describe the work of the Holy Spirit in three ways. First, the Spirit will convict the world of its wrongness in not believing in Jesus (verse 9). Secondly, the Spirit will convince people that Jesus has been in the right all along, by showing that Jesus goes to the Father – by receiving him, the Father vindicates the cause of Jesus (verse 10). And thirdly, the Spirit will convince the world about judgement because he will show that the prince of the world stands condemned (verse 11). It is Satan who is cast down and Jesus who is lifted up. The cross is not a victory for evil at all; rather, it is the place of evil's defeat.

## Christ over all   Ephesians 1.15 – 23

The letter to the Ephesians does not read in quite the same way as the other New Testament letters usually attributed to Paul. At times it is more sermonic, or like a doctrinal treatise. These and other matters have led some to question Paul's authorship but that is not our concern, so we shall call the author Paul. He is concerned to express and explore something of God's great plan that has found its focus in Christ (Ephesians 1.10).

After a passage of sustained blessing and praise of God for all his work and purpose in Christ (Ephesians 1.3 – 14), Paul moves to thanksgiving and intercession for the church at Ephesus. He knows of the faith and love of this church and for this he gives thanks to God. But he prays for more – that the church may grow in the knowledge of God. In particular, in verses 18 – 19, that they might know:

- the hope to which God calls them;
- the riches of their inheritance with the saints;
- the greatness of God's power.

Paul sees that power of God focused in Christ and, in particular, God's great work of raising Jesus from the dead. But we notice in verse 20 how resurrection is linked with ascension. Christ is exalted to the right hand of God, the place of authority. There are echoes here of Psalm 110.1 and Psalm 8.6. In the thought world of the time, not least in certain aspects of Judaism, there were levels or degrees of spiritual angelic beings who could be described as rule, authority, power and dominion. What Paul is claiming is that Christ is raised above all these, and not just for the present age but for all ages to come. Christ's exalted authority is for ever. There is no description of the ascension. But the belief that Jesus Christ, who shed his blood for us (Ephesians 1.7) and is now at the place of power and authority, is clearly part of the Church's proclamation.

Paul says in verse 22 that God has put all things under Christ's feet (another echo of Psalm 8.6) and made him head of the Church. The phrase that follows in verse 23, about 'the fullness of him who fills all in all' is particularly difficult to translate and understand. Among its many possible interpretations is the thought that Christ, being filled with the fullness of God, is both head of the Church as well as being fully in the Church as its life.

## The gifts of the ascended Lord   Ephesians 4.1–13

In the first three chapters of Ephesians Paul has been expounding insights into the great plan and purpose of God in Christ. It involves a new humanity, new social order, a new way of life. This part of the letter comes to a climax in a great benediction (3.20 – 21).

But Paul always follows his doctrinal writings with ethical consequences. So, Ephesians 4 opens up with a 'therefore'. Because of what God has done, because God has brought together what was separate, the Church must live a life worthy of the calling that is hers. Two marks in particular belong to the Christian Church – unity and holiness.

Christ has not simply called the Church into being and then abandoned it. Each member has received something from Christ (verse 7). Paul drives this point home with a quotation from Psalm 68.18. The verse in Ephesians speaks of God giving gifts to his people, while the Psalm verse, in contrast, has God receiving gifts from his people. Is this a deliberate change? Or has it happened almost unconsciously because the apostle is struck by how much Christ has given and how he goes on giving? Grace – the free saving gift of God – is a major theme of the letter.

Now Paul makes an important point. He understands the 'ascended one' to be Christ. But this is the same Christ who descended. This could either mean the incarnation of Christ, his coming down to earth, or his descent into hell. Either way, Paul is insisting that the one who descended – that Jesus of flesh and blood, the cross and the empty tomb – is the one who has ascended 'far above all the heavens' (verse 10).

His ascension is in order that he might 'fill all things'. It is not that the ascension therefore removes Christ from the earth but that rather in a more profound way Christ can be present everywhere. Ascension is not the removal of Christ from our world so much as creating the possibility that we might live in his.

The ascended Christ is the one who gives gifts. And his gifts are not things – money, wealth, property – but people, people whom he fills with his Spirit. These people are given to help the Church to live in its true calling. That calling is to belong to and be the body of Christ, so inclusive that in the end all of us come to a new humanity measured by nothing less than Christ himself. He has gone up. Into him we are called to grow up into 'the full stature of Christ' – and Christ himself helps us with his gifts.

## Some personal reflections

The ascension is an important Christian doctrine. It is there in the creeds. Even more it is there, implicitly or explicitly, in the New Testament. It is more fundamental to Christian belief than we normally recognise. In the concluding part of this chapter we shall direct our attention to four major implications of the doctrine. This will be far from a complete examination; but it will, hopefully, help us see further into the affirmation that 'he ascended into heaven' is good news.

We have noticed how, although Luke, John and Paul speak about ascension in different ways, none the less they understand that the resurrection and ascension of Jesus are inseparably linked. Indeed, the point has been often made that it is the same Jesus who went to the cross, was laid in the tomb, was raised from the dead, has ascended into heaven, and will come again.

Ascension is therefore seen in the New Testament as the divine 'Yes' to the life and death of Jesus. He had preached and lived the kingdom in the face of hostility, hatred and rejection. His opponents could even say that, far from being godly, he was demonic (Mark 3.22). He was put to death in a manner that would lead any Jew to believe he was cursed of God (see Deuteronomy 21.22 – 23).

But it is the crucified Jesus who is raised from the dead and who is taken up into heaven. His cause is vindicated by God in the face of his enemies. It is Jesus, not the powers and authorities of his day who come to share the company of God in glory. Ascension, with resurrection, is the vindication of the despised and crucified Lord.

We have also noted in the Bible readings how ascension is to 'the right hand of God'. This is a powerful symbol of authority. Jesus, who in the days of his flesh was subject to the dominion of Caesar, Pilate,

Caiaphas and the crowd, is now given all authority in heaven and on earth (Matthew 28.18).

Those who lived in New Testament times would have believed in principalities and powers, spiritual beings, who ruled their lives and shaped their destinies. As such, these powers were to be feared for no one could contain and control them. But Jesus has been raised and is ascended far above all principalities and powers. He has authority and dominion granted to him over these dark forbidding influences.

But what does this authority amount to? Are not all those forces that contrived to crucify Jesus still actively at work in the world? Yes, they are. But what ascension proclaims is that they do not have the final word. Their power is not ultimate. They are active only in this present age until finally they too will bow the knee before Christ. This means, however, that Christians can live confidently in the face of any challenge to their faith. If Christ had not ascended to the right hand of God then there might still be a struggle for ultimate authority over the affairs of earth. But God has spoken. Jesus is ascended. The power of principalities and powers is broken (see Ephesians 1.20 – 21 and 6.12). We can live confidently in Christ.

This is not to say that an easy triumphalism characterises Christian living. The end is not yet and there are still struggles to be endured in the cause of the kingdom of God. The costly call to be witnesses to Christ and his sovereignty is part of the resurrection story.

There is from time to time argument, both in and out of the Church, about the relationship between Christianity and politics. Should the Church keep out of politics? If we believe in the ascension then it is hard to see how we can avoid it. It has been said that the ascension is the most political of all the doctrines of the New Testament.

Why is this? Because it proclaims who is Lord – who has final authority and dominion. It calls us to live in the will of Jesus Christ and that can sometimes bring the Church into direct conflict with the will of the government. Let me give three illustrations of what I mean.

We are beginning to see important changes in the life of South Africa. In 1991, when I am writing this, it is still a long way from a genuine democracy that most of us would recognise where each person has the right to vote. At present, it is mostly only the white people who have that right. But apartheid, the policy of separated development of white and black people, is steadily being changed. There has always been a consistent challenge to the South African government's policy from Christians. Archbishop Desmond Tutu and Trevor Huddleston are just two of the best known of those who have realised that such a policy is utterly at odds with the teaching and will of Jesus Christ. They realised, costly as it might be, that if they believed that Jesus Christ is Lord then they must oppose this serious challenge to his kingdom. This inevitably took them into politics, not because they were first being political but because they were being Christian – that is, they were believing that Jesus Christ, risen and ascended, is **Lord**.

The second illustration is of a similar nature. It concerns the life and work of Martin Luther King. There was not the same kind of formal apartheid in the America of his experience as in South Africa, but there was active racism that was unjust and dehumanising. It was a power that stood against the rule of Christ and, tragically, it could be found in the churches. Martin Luther King found that, in the name of the gospel of Jesus the Lord, he had to take his stand. He began to work with other Christians, and those of no religious persuasion at all, to do battle with the sin of racism. His great 'I have a dream' speech proclaimed his faith. He knew that the cause of Christ would triumph. Evil cannot finally stand against it. He died for his beliefs but his death only extended the social, political and spiritual influence of this deeply religious man.

The third illustration comes from Germany and the years just before the Second World War. Hitler had come to power and was intent on making Germany great again after the humiliation of the First World War defeat. He managed to rouse great patriotism and nationalism in his rise to power and in this many Christians gave him support.

However, gradually there arose strong opposition from those who became known as the Confessing Church. They saw Hitler's work as being corrupt, ideological and contrary to the cause of Christ. Nationalism can become idolatrous when a totalitarian leadership oversteps the legitimate demands of the state. So, largely under the influence of Karl Barth, a statement of the Confessing Church was drawn up at the Synod of Barmen in 1934. It affirmed that Jesus Christ alone is the living word of God; he alone is the Lord who can claim absolute obedience. Many of those who shared this conviction soon suffered for their stand. Barth lost his professor's post at Bonn University. Dietrich Bonhoeffer was eventually imprisoned and hanged. These and others did not seek a political cause but their faithful obedience to the conviction that the risen and ascended Christ is Lord led them along the path of conflict, even to martyrdom. To confess Christ as Lord is to make a statement with potentially great political consequences.

Finally, the ascension of Jesus means the out-pouring of the Holy Spirit and the enabling of the Church's mission under God. This is a point made most clearly in John's Gospel. The Spirit can only be given when Jesus is glorified. In his going the Church receives the gift we could not receive before. So, as was illustrated in Luke's writings, the end is but a beginning; the going of Jesus makes possible the coming of the Spirit.

It means that as heaven touched earth in the incarnation, so that contact is maintained, in two senses. Jesus has taken our humanity, the humanity he shared, into the presence of God. And yet God is still among us in the Spirit.

When we looked at the Gospels we saw that there was a special link between the risen Jesus and the awareness of his presence by the Church at the Holy Communion Service or Eucharist. Here is a foretaste of what is to come when all things, in heaven and on earth, are gathered up into Christ and he is all in all.

Until then, confessing the risen and ascended Jesus as Lord, the Church lives in hopeful confident witness by the power of the Spirit.

**A prayer**

You have gone from us, Lord,
and yet we are not sad.
You could not have stayed with us for ever.
You had to go
or we would never have grown up.
You had to go
or the Spirit would not have been given.
You had to go
to pioneer the way to glory.
So we praise you, risen, ascended Lord.
To you the Father has given all authority,
and we are glad.
Who else could ever be worthy
    of such trust and honour?
Who else could we trust with such dominion?
You are Lord,
We confess this truth in baptism.
We celebrate you at each Communion.
By your Spirit
help us to confess and celebrate you
in all our living
in the way we speak,
                spend,
                plan,
                vote.
In all our choosing and living,
be our freedom,
be our Saviour,
be our Lord.

**Some questions and suggestions for further thought**

1 What would you say to the person who claimed that Christians should stay out of politics?

2 Think hard about your own life. Be as honest as you can about those aspects of your living that need to be more obviously under the lordship of Christ than they are.

3 The first Christians spoke of the exaltation of Christ in spatial metaphors of 'ascending' or 'being taken up'. Can you think of other ways in which we can proclaim the same gospel?

4 How could your church celebrate the ascension in its worship this year? Think about ways of worship that will help your church to hear this gospel message.